The Anti-Booklist

The Anti-Booklist

**Edited by Brian Redhead
and Kenneth McLeish**

Cartoons by Michael Heath

HODDER AND STOUGHTON
LONDON   SYDNEY   AUCKLAND   TORONTO

Most of the bibliographical information in this book has been taken from *Books in Print 1980*. Where possible the original date of publication and the most recently available edition (with its date) have been given. We have tried to ensure that this information is correct, but apologise if there are any inaccuracies.

British Library Cataloguing in Publication Data
Redhead, Brian and McLeish, Kenneth (eds.)
The Anti-booklist.
  1. Bibliography
  I. Redhead, Brian II. McLeish, Kenneth
  011   Z1003

  ISBN 0 340 27084 5
  ISBN 0 340 27447 6 Pbk

Phototypesetting by Swiftpages Limited, Liverpool.
Printed in Great Britain for Hodder and Stoughton Limited, Mill Road, Dunton Green, Sevenoaks, Kent by Richard Clay (The Chaucer Press) Ltd, Bungay, Suffolk.

Hodder and Stoughton Editorial Office: 47 Bedford Square, London WC1B 3DP.

CONTENTS

Introduction		7
Jeffrey Archer	THE SPELL OF WORDS	9
Beryl Bainbridge	AFRAID OF FREUD	11
Patricia Beer	UNBEARABLE	13
Diana Bishop	THE PROSECUTION RESTS BUT THE ACTOR NEEDS THE WORK	15
Basil Boothroyd	NAMING OF PARTS	18
Caroline Conran	NOTHING TO LOSE	20
Alan Coren	TWO WONDERLOAVES, FIVE FISH FINGERS	22
Russell Davies	PLEASUREBUBBLE HUBBYHOUSE	24
Frank Delaney	SEE PAGE 285 . . .	26
Janice Elliott	SHEER FUDGE	28
Michael Green	CAPTAIN HORATION RAMAGE	30
Alex Hamilton	ENRICHING DIET	32
Tim Heald	MISSING PERSONS	34
Robert Heller	BECAUSE OF THE MINTS	36
Bevis Hillier	AN UNFUNNY THING HAPPENED TO ME	38
Michael Holroyd	THE SOUND OF BUBBLES	41
Roland Huntford	LITTLE ÁRPÁD	43
Brian Inglis	CRADLE AND ALL	45
David Irving	THE X + 1 PHENOMENON	47
D.A.N. Jones	BITTER PLUMS	49
H.R.F. Keating	DAGGER IN THE BACK	51
Miles Kington	HER ARMS AKIMBO	53
Paul Levy	COOKING: THE BOOKS	57
George MacBeth	WITHOUT A PLOT	59
Kenneth McLeish	HEM, HEM	61
Fay Maschler	PRETTY THIN	64
Sheridan Morley	NOT GOOD FOR YOU	66

Charles Osborne	BACKFIRED	68
John Osborne	GRIEVOUS BODILY HARM	70
Steve Race	SNOBBERY WITH VIOLENCE	74
Frederic Raphael	AUTHORISED VERSION	76
Brian Redhead	TO HAVE OR HAVE NOT	79
Stanley Reynolds	LOS CRAPOS	81
Hilary Rubinstein	UNCLEAN! UNCLEAN!	84
Michael Schmidt	SHADOWY PUPPETS	86
Audrey Slaughter	SECOND-HAND SWORD	88
Anne Smith	THE LADY AND THE TRAMP	91
Anthony Smith	TEXTUAL CRITICISM	94
Godfrey Smith	MADNESS, DO YOU HEAR?	97
John Timpson	WHY IT NEVER GOT OUT	99
Peter Tinniswood	WE CAN'T HAVE ONE	102
Polly Toynbee	DEAR SUPERWOMAN	104
John Vaizey	TWEE TROLLEY	107
Robert Waterhouse	VANITY MIRROR	110
Harry Whewell	THOUGHT, WORD AND DEED	112
Charles Wood	THE UNKINDEST CUT	114
Ian Wooldridge	SLANT-EYED ORIENTAL	120
One Man's Meat		122
Biographical Detail		125
Index of Titles and Authors		131

INTRODUCTION

This book sprang from a BBC Radio programme suggested by Kenneth McLeish and called *The Titanic Book List*. In it Brian Redhead invited three people to nominate the books they would like to have seen go down in the *Titanic* and to discuss their reasons why.

Redhead himself was rude about Tolkien, quoting Edmund Wilson: "his appeal is to readers with a lifelong appetite for juvenile trash", but would not hear a word against Nabokov on the grounds that *Lolita* contains one of the great sentences of all literature. It comes in the passage in which Miss Pratt, the headmistress, is censuring Humbert Humbert for his bad influence on Lolita, saying things like: "We insist you un-veto her non-participation in the dramatic group," and Nabokov has HH think this to himself: "Should I marry Pratt and strangle her?"

McLeish admitted that he had been a founder member of the Tolkien cult at the age of sixteen, that he had read him eight times altogether, and abruptly couldn't stand him any longer. *The Lord of the Rings*, he argued, was not a parable of good and evil, but a boys'-own-paper-science-fiction story. Frodo and Sam were just Biggles and Algy trapped in someone else's time warp.

Patricia Beer looked askance at Dorothy L. Sayers (the later works) finding them irresponsible in the use of language and in her translation of Dante grotesque. John Drummond, delicately and with no desire to offend, nonetheless dismissed all twelve volumes of Anthony Powell's *Dance to the Music of Time* because in them nothing actually happens.

Miss Beer disagreed. Were the works of Powell to go down in the *Titanic*, she would go down in a wet suit and read them on the seabed.

The response of listeners to the programme was

passionate, ranging from angry admonition – "How dare you associate yourself with such a wicked enterprise?" – to liberated praise – "I have thought that for years but have never dared to say it out loud."

Gillian Reynolds, writing in the *Daily Telegraph*, said that there was a certain curious satisfaction in hearing an anti-celebration on Radio 4, for once, but she thought we might have acknowledged which old newspaper column first gave us the idea. Research revealed that ten years earlier Stanley Reynolds, in his column in the *Guardian*, had produced not only a *Titanic* Book List but a Play List, a Film List – almost an Endless List. Stanley graciously agreed to contribute to this book.

Paul Ferris in the *Observer* thought the idea should be extended to radio programmes — *The Archers* even. And when an anonymous correspondent wrote, saying, "Why not a *Titanic* Lloyds List?" Redhead and McLeish decided there must be a book in it, an opinion shared by the first publisher they asked.

When, however, they began to approach possible contributors to this book the response was very mixed. Some had their contributions in by return of post; others thought the very idea pernicious and philistine. Some could not think of any books they actually disliked. "That," wrote Robert Robinson, "makes me a very sweet person." Some could not bring themselves to speak unkindly of a fellow author. "The writing of any book, however bad," wrote Anthony Burgess, "is too agonising for the flippant dismissal that seems implied." Some were simply loyal. "I am," wrote Fay Weldon, "a fully paid-up member of the Writers' Guild of Great Britain." Some would not do it for the money. "The pay," wrote Kingsley Amis, "is too depressing." Erica Jong was fiercely anti: "In an age of declining literacy, widespread hostility to books and authors, the last thing we need is an anti-book."

But most enthused and contributed, conscious, as one of them observed, that the books assailed here will never get a better press.

JEFFREY ARCHER
The Spell of Words

I detest the *Pocket Oxford Dictionary of the English Language* because I can't spell, so when I try to look up a word I can never find it. I hate the *Concise Oxford Dictionary of Current English* because it has far too many words my wife keeps using and I have to try and find out what they mean. I loath the *Shorter Oxford English Dictionary* because it is a missnomer (see what I mean about my spelling) there is nothing short about these two volumes and the editors should be put on trial under the Trade Descriptions Act. As for the *Oxford English Dictionary*, although some fool gave me all fourteen volumes as a gift I can never imagine a situation arising where I would need to look up a word that wasn't in the *Pocket Oxford Dictionary*.

Dr Atkins' Diet Revolution has taught me how to take off seven pounds in seven days and *Delia Smith's Cookery Course* has shown me how to put it back on in one day, so both Dr Atkins and Miss Smith should be burnt at the stake (along with their books) like medevl witches.

My agent Debbie was foolish enough to marry Dr David Owen so I have to plough through his books (they are always very long and very expensive). *The Henry Root Letters* are quite despicable (he never wrote to me), and I wish my mother had discovered (or written?) *Country Diary of an Edwardian Lady*. I consider it quite obscene to be on the bestsellers' list for over three years.

Finally, *War and Peace* maddens me because I didn't write it myself, and worse, I couldn't.

Pocket Oxford Dictionary of the English Language, *OUP*, 1978

Concise Oxford Dictionary of Current English, *OUP, 1964*

Shorter Oxford English Dictionary, *OUP, 1973*

Oxford English Dictionary, *OUP, 1933*

Robert C. Atkins, Dr. Atkins' Diet Revolution, *Bantam, 1974*

Delia Smith, Cookery Course, Parts 1, 2 and 3, *BBC, 1978, 1979, 1981*

David Owen, ed, A Unified Health Service, *Pergamon, 1968*

David Owen, In Sickness and in Health, *Quartet, 1976*

David Owen, Face the Future, *Cape, 1981*

The Henry Root Letters *(Weidenfeld and Nicolson, 1980), Futura, 1981*

Edith Holden, Country Diary of an Edwardian Lady, *Michael Joseph and Webb and Bower, 1977*

Leo Tolstoy, War and Peace *(first published 1866), Pan, 1972*

BERYL BAINBRIDGE
Afraid of Freud

I have tried to think of a novel that I wouldn't mind being sunk without trace, and failed. I don't finish books I don't like. I did imagine *Plexus* by Henry Miller might qualify but, after reading it through to the end, changed my mind. Parts of it are awful, some of it is not. At any rate it gave me bad dreams, or rather a nightmare, and it was this that made me remember Freud. Every Friday night, years ago in Liverpool, I used to discuss Poetry and Life with my lodger Harry, and an elderly Jewish lady called Leah. I've not discussed either subject since, but when I left Liverpool for the South, Harry and Leah bought me a copy of Freud's *The Interpretation of Dreams*. I read it, on and off, for five years, and so feel justified in saying it could well be dispensed with altogether.

In his preface to the second edition, and carelessly cutting out one half of the human race, the author wrote that he thought the book was a portion of his own self-analysis, a reaction to his father's death: "that is to say, to the most important event, the most poignant loss in a man's life. Having discovered that this was so, I felt unable to obliterate the traces of this experience." He goes on somewhat optimistically to conclude that to his readers, however, it would be a matter of indifference upon what particular material they learned to appreciate the importance of dreams and how to interpret them. And that's precisely the rub. One can hardly be indifferent to a syllable uttered by Freud. The entire world changed because of him. Until he came along there were still such things as good people and bad people. Practically single-handed he got rid of sin and evil. To be fair to him, he does say once or twice in his preface to the sixth or seventh edition of his book that not every blessed dream has a sexual basis, just most of them. He says it's because we were all suppressed in childhood by our nursemaids who were either extorting us to pull down our nightgowns or doing lewd things to us in the bath. Who, for instance, he asks, would suspect the presence of a sexual element in the dream of a little house with closed doors? Who would imagine that dreaming of one's wife leading one towards the little house with the closed doors and slipping quickly inside, would have a sexual wish behind it? Who indeed, pre-Freud?

I have a feeling that none of us dream much any more, and when we do the little doors are wide open. We're not suppressed enough and it's all been explained. Without Freud we could have lived out our shifty days in peace and filled our guilty nights with dreams.

Henry Miller, Plexus *(first published 1953), Panther, 1969*
Sigmund Freud, The Interpretation of Dreams *(first*
published 1900), Penguin, 1976

PATRICIA BEER

Unbearable

In denouncing F. R. Leavis's *New Bearings in English Poetry,* I suppose I'm really too late; the damage has been done. Or, alternatively, I may be locking the door of a stable in which there never was a steed. But it will be a satisfaction nevertheless.

F. R. Leavis's talent was essentially a talent to abuse. And the Leavisites have inherited and in some cases developed this gift, for as in all religions the disciples have tended to make more mischief than the Master himself.

My grievance is that Leavis taught a whole generation to sneer. Everybody has, I imagine, the right to sneer if he really needs to, but positively to teach other people to sneer seems to me immoral. *New Bearings* came out in 1932; and in the 1940s, when I was at university, it was exercising a great and malign influence.

Anybody who could call Thomas Hardy "a naive poet of simple attitudes and outlook" needs watching for a start. But Leavis's weapon against Hardy was really nothing worse than perfunctoriness. His real attack was directed at the great earlier Victorians. For Tennyson to have achieved his poetic ambitions, we are told, he would have had to possess "a much finer intelligence, a much more robust original genius, much greater strength and courage" than he had. Well, now we know: Tennyson was thick, derivative, weak and cowardly. Perhaps Browning comes off better. Not so, I'm afraid. "So inferior a mind and spirit as Browning's could not provide the impulse needed to bring back into poetry the adult intelligence." And all this, mind you, from a critic who never wrote a successful line of poetry in his life.

He did no harm to Tennyson and Browning, we may be sure. Whatever their actual shape and substance may have been in 1932, they probably cried all their way to the pantheon. And one should add in fairness that much of the book is relatively harmless, consisting mostly of dotty prophecies and pathological blind spots.

But he did considerable harm to me. Eighteen-year-old students in my time were more susceptible to intellectual bullying than are those of today; and the agony of hearing my favourite poets and companions – for I was a bookish child – mocked and derided, brutally and without reasoned explanation, is something I can't forgive or forget.

I don't know how much influence Leavis wields today. Still quite a bit, I should have thought. In case he wields *any*, please publish my sentiments.

F. R. Leavis, New Bearings in English Poetry (first published 1932), Penguin, 1972

DIANA BISHOP

The Prosecution Rests
But the Actor Needs the Work

Having gone so far as to take the plays of A. Christie out of the library to remind myself why, since those distant repertory days, I have remembered them with such hatred, after many false starts and swift glances (but not so many as in the texts) I knew. Everything about them is quite unspeakable, not least the dialogue. However, they are actor-proof since good or even brilliant actors appear uniformly mediocre.

There is one play, for example, in which in order for the characters to move about the stage at all they have to smoke themselves to death. There are over seventy stage directions immediately concerned with smoking. ("She fetches ashtray", "He moves to stub out his cigarette" etc.) Some poor director was obviously faced with the problem endemic in the writing that once a character appears through an archway or a french window or even, *in extremis,* a door, there is nothing remotely logical left in the text for him to say or do. Or her. A. Christie makes great play, if not great plays, of the phrase "or her".

Let us take the case of the actress – no, I'm confusing you – let us consider the actress the least of whose worries will be that she is called upon to "react imperceptibly". Any actress who can stand still and express nothing at all at this point will walk away with the evening. Not so fortunate the actor who must "sidle suspiciously towards the door". He has possibly managed to work out that he is not the murderer, indeed that he is wholly innocent. Nevertheless he has to motivate himself in character along the backdrop. Perhaps the character needs a pee and is suspicious of the quality of the country-house plumbing.

Now it is fair enough for one of the protagonists to be a homicidal maniac – he is the murderer and quite simple to play. But the other roles are of merely common-or-garden maniacs. They behave oddly or say extraordinary things for no reason which is obvious to the actor (frequently sane – at least at the beginning of the run).

DONALD   I may be a thief, a robber (He moves slowly towards Mollie) a fugitive from justice – a madman – even – a murderer!

MOLLIE   (Backing away) Oh.

She may well say oh. What else can you say when someone moves slowly towards you spouting such pretentious rubbish? She could offer him a cigarette, I suppose.

Then there is the problem of how best to serve the wit and subtlety of the writing, but this at least can be easily shelved as there is none. Neither is there any characterisation; all the speeches sound alike. Any actor can say any other actor's lines. In fact they often do. Sometimes the text instructs them to, as in one play where three quite different characters say, "You startled me." When in doubt while playing in any piece by A. Christie say, "You startled me." Usually you will be right. Not only will the character be startled but also the actor, particularly if he has heard a correct cue, since all the lines are a) unlearnable and b) instantly forgettable. Let me explain how you can forget that which you have never known. Firstly, at rehearsal, the actors say to the director, "Look, Peter, I can't possibly say this. No one talks like this." So the line is changed into English. But then because the plot is so absurdly unlikely the actors forget the lines they have substituted.

So the scene with Jemima (or whoever) and the Inspector goes like this:

INSPECTOR   Now then, what really did happen this evening?

JEMIMA   Er – er – I – er – (She looks desperately at the Inspector)

INSPECTOR   (Wondering if she is acting) Yes, Mrs Fanworth-Smith?

JEMIMA   (Pleading with her eyes) Don't you know, Inspector?

INSPECTOR (Heaving a deep sigh) Well, was it something like this? You said goodbye to Ferdinand and he'd gone off with Miss Beale. You didn't know Angus would come back again and you still can't understand why he did. Then your Uncle came home, explaining he would have to go out again immediately. He went off in the car and it was just after you shut the front door that you began to feel nervous. (Jemima sinks onto settee with relief.)

JEMIMA Yes. That's right.

INSPECTOR (Hopefully) Why?

JEMIMA Why? Er – erm –

INSPECTOR (Clenching his teeth) Oh my God! It occurred to you you'd never been in the house alone at night.

JEMIMA Oh yes.

You can see that eventually the actor playing the Inspector will have a nervous breakdown, but that does not matter since A. Christie's inspectors often do, particularly in those of her plays in which he is also the murderer or the victim who is really pretending to be dead or him (or her).

But what is the worst aspect of it all, the really horrifying thing about these nightly trials which turn actors into speechless, stumbling wrecks?

They make money, and audience – may God forgive them, for actors won't – love them.

Agatha Christie, Afternoon at the Seaside, *French*
Akhnaton: A Play in Three Acts, *Collins, 1973*
The Mousetrap, *French, 1978*
A Murder is Announced, *French, 1978*
Murder on the Nile, *French*
Spider's Web, *French*
Ten Little Niggers, *French*
Towards Zero, *French*
The Unexpected Guest, *French*
Witness for the Prosecution, *French*

BASIL BOOTHROYD

Naming of Parts

Nobody knows what the Turks did to T. E. Lawrence at Bashim-el-Butum, if I have the name right, and if that's where they did it, whatever it was. In adaptations of *Seven Pillars of Wisdom* for stage and screen, to the best of my sand-blinded recollection, this piece of drama takes place off scene, and actors interpreting the central character come on when it's over, staggering into view looking upset and chalky.

When I say nobody knows – apart, perhaps, from a few wistfully geriatric Turks – I mean no one who hasn't read the Pillars. Which I haven't, myself, though not for the want of trying.

A friend, hitherto accepted as truthful, says he's read every word, or all 275,000. When I asked if he'd read words like Snainirat, Mukheymer and Thlaithukwhat, he muttered something and went off to whip through *War and Peace* in his coffee-break. My guess is that when he came to words like that he just said to himself, "Oh, that", and hopped a few lines until his pronunciation buds had simmered down.

Moreover, if he did read them, I bet he couldn't tell me now whether they were people, places or camels. Considering that Lawrence was setting trains on fire most of the time, when he wasn't telling Allenby where to get off, or planning to release his book in dribs and drabs so as to spare the public too much genius at one swallow, he did well to get his notes down.

He clearly did, though, otherwise he could have confused the exact nature of the sunset over Gasem el Shimt on 19th June with the way particular camels knelt down on your average Shrove Tuesday. He packs the stuff in all right. And when you remember he lost the first draft on Reading station, a rotten place for it to happen, and "scribbled it out again", as he modestly puts it, in

Paris, you can't say his eye for detail wasn't OK.

I don't want to belittle him. He never did. Why should I? Any humble, young, and unmilitary archaeologist would impress himself, getting up to the larks he did. I mean, think. Came out fighting from the British Museum, and in no time rose to a World War I colonel, rushing about in amusing headgear and shooting people.

My friend with the voracious literary maw wouldn't tell me what the Turks did. He pretended he had to get through *Decline and Fall* before bedtime. I don't think he knew, frankly, but it remains a point of interest for me, and if only, by leafing through the five or six hundred pages and just hitting on it, I could get it cleared up, I could take the book round to my second-hand dealer and ask what offers.

Meanwhile, I'm starting at the back end again. This is often the quickest way with detective stories. The indices of place and personal names are pretty good, if you can pronounce any of them, and the fully documented nominal roll of the Hejaz Armoured Car Company and the Ten-Pounder Talbot Battery – ten-pounders, my God, that's what I call fire-power – is enough to make your endpapers stand on end.

How are your wrists? If they hold up while you're holding this, and you come across . . . you know, that bit where the Turks insulted his mother, or fed him chunks of rancid Delight . . . drop me a line, right? Keep the length down, though. It's just the simple, amazing facts I'm after.

T. E. Lawrence, Seven Pillars of Wisdom (*first published 1926*), *Penguin*

Leo Tolstoy, War and Peace (*first published 1866*), *Pan. 1972*

Edward Gibbon, Decline and Fall of the Roman Empire (*first published 1776*), *Penguin, 1972*

CAROLINE CONRAN

Nothing to Lose

The Female Eunuch was a book I didn't much enjoy. I never felt down-trodden before I read it and if anyone stepped on me I could tell them to stop. I had always thought, like Joan Didion (whose book *The White Album* I did enjoy), that "nobody forces women to buy the package." But since reading this pernicious book, which I did a year ago, ten years later than anyone else, I have found people queuing up to take advantage of me. Rough misogynistical lads on building-sites damage my ego by whistling and calling out derisively, reducing me to a mere object. My job, although rather enjoyable and well paid, is, as I now realise, spurious since it involves writing about nothing more important than cooking: the sort of rubbishy, menial subject that only a woman who hasn't realised herself could possibly be boring enough to bother with. I used to thinking cooking was a deliciously creative and useful pastime, but of course Germaine Greer points out that one is really just serving as an unpaid skivvy. And my cleaning ladies and I used to have a good chat over cups of tea, making fun of our husbands' peculiarities – alas, thanks to Germaine the once easily tolerated peculiarities have become glaring male chauvinist faults, no longer to be put up with but opposed. Farewell to harmony, I must put my partner right on a number of scores. He can't expect me to have a job *and* look after the children *and* shop *and* cook the supper. Never mind if I once enjoyed it and found it comfortable – now it's exploitation, Germaine says so. If I can't get these jobs shared out, if I can't be as hairy-legged and grumpy as my husband, what possible good can there be in my being alive at all?

There is a saying of I Ching, on which I base very few aspects of my life, that if the weak oppose the strong head-on, the weak can't win, but both will be injured.

This is I think a rather good comment, but who are the weak? Feminine strength has always been as Christopher Booker is quoted as saying, "feeling and intuition . . . the intuitive spiritual dimension of life – that intangible thing we call soul," while masculine strength represents "power and order, structure and discipline". When women start to take on masculine characteristics, then they become as strong-minded and insensitive as any man – look at Mrs Thatcher and Mrs Gandhi – very disappointing. Ms Greer is not actually suggesting that women should become like men, only more like themselves, more like people. But if, as she *does* suggest, they try and do it in the way that men do, by being tough and demanding, it's going to be a poor prospect for everyone. Women surely have so much to offer as they are, with their own particular natures (and difficulties) that it seems a pity that they are expected to change, and take on masculine characteristics just to get their foot in the door.

Another question raised in my mind by Germaine Greer is, "What is it all for?" Having rid oneself of the shackles of responsibility for home and family, presumably one then has to assume the nine-to-five shackles in order to earn enough to live on. Unless one actually has a total dedication to some artistic self-expression or other fulfilling endeavour, one is simply committing oneself to different institutions. And probably, having sorted out one's own personality and become very, very free of dependence on others, unless one is actually an artist who *must* write, paint or perform, one is left with a very empty life at the end of it all.

Germaine Greer, The Female Eunuch *(first published 1970)*, *Paladin, 1971*
Joan Didion, The White Album, *Weidenfeld and Nicolson*, *1979*

ALAN COREN

Two Wonderloaves, Five Fish Fingers

"In the beginning was the Word, and the Word was with God, and the Word was God."

By 1947, however, the Word was with the Joint Committee on the New Translation of the Bible; who, hurling themselves upon it with all the creative zeal and poetic sensibility one would naturally expect from the combined literary imaginations of twelve separate panels of ecclesiastical and academic advisers, took only twenty-three years to come up with a new Authorised Version which was as spectacular and exciting an advance over its tatty predecessor as the wondrous Centre Point is over the grimy excrescence of Salisbury Cathedral.

In short, the Good Book disappeared, to reappear as the Bad Book; as resurrections go, the Church has experienced better. Few who have read it have expressed surprise that the man who masterminded it should have signed the preface with an assumed name, but as one of those who knows the true identity of Donald Ebor, I shall allow proper charity to seal my lips.

Why is the *New English Bible* so dreadful? Let us hand it its own petard, and see how it copes with the opening sentence shared by me and St John:

"When all things began, the Word already was. The Word dwelt with God, and what God was, the Word was."

There is, is there not, a sort of brilliance there? Some translators are able to remove all sense from their original, some are able to remove all style, some are able to remove all originality; but it takes, surely, a genius simultaneously to remove all three. A committee capable of taking a sentence which climaxed on *God* and rehashing it into a sentence which climaxes on *was* is no ordinary committee. You have to be born that way.

As desecrators, the Joint Committee leave the Visigoths at the post: sack a temple, and the congregation may still stand in an open field and worship, provided you have left them the verbal wherewithal. But the Joint Committee have removed the life from the word: mystery has been replaced with confusion, magic has been replaced with conjuring, poetry has been replaced with jargon. There is more to communion than communication, and more to meaning than saying.

And infinitely (a word chosen, I promise, with far greater care than the Joint Committee ever deployed) more depressing than the mere awfulness of the NEB is the fact that this is no ordinary bestseller to be tossed in the Gatwick bin after its hour's diversion is discharged; it is a bestseller that will continue to best-sell long after the Joint Committee has gone to dust and Donald Ebor has finished explaining to his Maker why he saw his temporal task as translating Holy Writ into a Government White Paper. Worse, the NEB is now the standard school text; and even if you want your kids to believe in nothing more than the immortality of English prose, that is very bad news indeed.

New English Bible (*first published 1961*), CUP, 1970

RUSSELL DAVIES

Pleasurebubble Hubbyhouse

Cobblears, I queek, con naught con all. This is a mis-
begoblin effart from swive of wive to brickfist type and
four pines ninetofive in any buddy's monure. Where's
your woollen tears, I asp yo, to be token by're lurke-wake
root sexhundread pagan laing (in your Fibre papalbag)
back to Head Case Engineering, wench we came. (No
anchor was the stern reply.)

Finagles Waste, bejamers joist, cannondrum in
excresis, insproats a crumplicadent nexicon of dump-
stincts withim yr fightful reportwire. He sews seemseeds
in the earshell (moultigreyed). Echo homo, littlesurs!
Yet in the upperroof of our puerole Humptyhead, alass,
wee stans a ghost. All tug Heather now, Here Comes
Excess! (Nutting degrees like digress, my old donski use
to shay, God press his iddle-gotten saul.) Well a big fat
darty booker it is to be Shaw, and I wouldn't have the
spiers to be waterlogging all the arks and chunderment
of openprism reduxdiseased betwee these greeny backs,
so geld me Hobson. Suffixit touche, o gintill redrum, it's
oh, allerline schoolerschrift filluphaben in a therasputin
donghell incarnabine. (Otis lifteywater I must dyke for it,
Father, plash me for I have skimmed. Or shuteye see,
flush me, Farber, for I am skint? Hamsters on a boast-
cart, please.)

I'll not abound to say you won't fine yourself tungling
over the odd tibs and bogs that hueffer to the kyries mine
pleasurebubble sensehavens of interlarkin dizzypins.
Not at Hall, the very tort of it is anaspirin for Deloittes of
me. Old Joys is a low-undo-himself. (And don't wee all.)
Notwithshandy he guts no eyes with ewers drooling.
And why should he, Gott safes the Mark, we cannot all
be Hainault Hobcecils scrimbling lists of the midevil
sainsburys, we'd all go roust the twins.

But, you interplate (those of you in whom the shap of

egremont is heather rising, gold blast you sirs, would you heave the price of a Riles-Royals about yez?) this is no rumtomb teararts billyphant from the Dully Bullygraft! This is Highly Charged Engrishe or I'm a touchmum! How ripe you are, penine interlexapples, I bough to your supearier fudgement. But are you shaun, are you dolgelly convicted we are dwelling with a Wort of Ark and not a Pickforth's vain of finto seems belunging to a literarty hen's teeth diva? Hom? You mistumblestand the jeskin? Swerve you right, you anchor! (Part my fringe.)

In the embolism comes it doubt to this: Filigrees Whelk, bejams juice, is a bleeding grant for pores, a hubbyhouse for the aldebarans of the acadome, och it's an obsolate codgeree of your hockmugrandiose christable prankhearse, and all the finn in it is in the parting together (on Joisus' path) and biggerole in the pollenasonder by ourshelf, misteral stingers that we bee. Sore knackers to Sham and Shawn! Annie Luvya Liverpool a la long term! Abbasso profungus in arsepick! Flaherty-o for the Missus! (The remarque is out of plays, I withdrawl it entimely with sunblest apollogrease.)

Now *Boatrace of the Hearties as a Ying Yang,* on the upperham, I meal your *Potroast of the Hartebeeste as a Yorke Ham,* ah yer *Prostitute of the Alldust as our Yon Mahon,* well that's a dufferin Cathal O'Fish altargodder. Innis?

James Joyce, Finnegans Wake *(first published 1939), Faber, 1975*

FRANK DELANEY

See Page 285 . . .

Is it spurious to select a book which I have never read? But that is precisely why I have selected it. That is to say, I have read it but I have not read it. I imagine that some clarification is required immediately.

Because of its general notoriety – hyperbolic in church-starched Ireland — *Lady Chatterley's Lover* was one of those books which circulated pruriently in school. And piecemeal – under the desks. The boy who had a complete chapter intact, rather than a page or two at a time, was a friend: the one who lent in substantial part (page 162 to the end of the American Grove edition) became a confidant. And so it came to pass that, irritatingly, I have not read, and am now unable to read, an entire continuous text of Lady C. Try as I will, the pages fall open among the forget-me-nots on page 285 (I now possess a full, undamaged copy of the American Grove edition). Oh, I could argue that I've missed little of the flavour of the book. Buds, hatching-eggs, fern, dripping naked trees (etc.), fluffy chickens, pinks, bluebells and brown blankets – Lawrence's sensuality came across in slivers. There were new words with meaning – and words with new meanings: schoolboy invective suddenly sounded ridiculous, needed adjusting in the face and light of Mellor's glossary of single syllables (no more than two words, but my! – how effective, and individual).

But such haphazard reading distorted at least one necessary literary value. Shakespeare must have been a committed marrying man. With the exception of Falstaff who did not exhibit a tendency to marry? But was Lawrence? I do not know for certain. Admittedly a reading of his biographies and other related works give clues. But now, do I prefer the jagged energies and stained-glass impressions of him which have accumulated from my hot moieties of Lady Chatterley?

My last objection to the book's continued presence in the world is my principal one. Coitus interruptus reading has been a difficult habit to break. I know as much of Harold Robbins and Radclyffe Hall and Frank Harris and Henry Miller and John Cleland and Boccaccio as I do of D. H. Lawrence. Now the only books which I am competent to read straight through are either those which I already know to be without forget-me-nots (if you get my meaning) or those sight unseen previously, but from whose demeanour I do not expect forget-me-nots. I can only read John Updike's *Couples* under a desk, Erica Jong's *Fear of Flying* in individual torn-out pages, Edna O'Brien and Norman Mailer behind somebody's bicycle shed. Therefore I want to abolish *Lady Chatterley's Lover*.

Lady Chatterley's Lover *was first published in subscription form from D. H. Lawrence's home in Florence in 1928, in expurgated form also in 1928, unabridged in Paris in 1929.*
Full free publication in England in 1960 (available in Penguin, 1969)
John Updike, Couples *(first published in the UK, 1968), Penguin, 1970*
Erica Jong, Fear of Flying *(first published in the UK, 1974), Panther, 1976*

JANICE ELLIOTT
Sheer Fudge

Letter from Virginia Woolf to her sister, Vanessa Bell, 1981

> Wood of the Suicides
> 7th Circle,
> Hell

Dearest,

What *do* you think of all this pitterpatter about us? All these books — do you not feel *industrialised*? They were bound to happen, of course, but they do remind me of that terrible dinner of Rose Macaulay's when Leonard beat his soup bowl violently & the talk was all so small. (I bought a slightly flawed herring in Soho this morning for only 2½d & then wondered if I should wait for the sales, it would have fallen further.)

But these biographies & memoirs, how they do go on: one feels like a fish in a school. (On the other hand there was haddock at 6d, smoked.) Now Ottoline has a book to herself alone, she is more herself than I think I can bear. And that nonsense concocted about Lytton by these baldnecked chicken! As L. says, sheer fudge. If he kept mice in his beard that would be Carrington's fault. Cheese no doubt, and her off with Partridge leaving Lytton to brush his own beard.

If this gossip must be spread, Quentin, I suppose, was fair if indiscreet & that Holroyd boy. But how they do go on as though we were no better than Miss Macaulay's dinner guests, speaking of nothing. (Now I know you don't agree that she shines, but I went over to Vita in the shay. Morgan was there & the Trefusis person & conversation was, as usual, of sodomy and sapphism. Brilliant. They were translucent. I felt dowdy. *Why* do you not care for my hair curled?)

Nigel in his little souvenirs very sweet about childhood meetings — I handed back to him & to Ben, he says, diamonds when they gave me lumps of coal. (Looking up and down, everywhere, for coke, all I could find in Oxford Street was coal so came home with a cod. I think of buying fish & remember my old signal of disaster, the fin rising on a wide blank sea. Madness and work – how strange they should still be with me. Sheer fudge, L. used to say of immortality, yet here we are, on the same old battlefield. Poor Carrington, naturally, awaited me.)

Perhaps if they left us in peace, we might rest? Our works – oh yes, I confess, I am vain enough to have them live. But how many now read Quentin and never a word of *The Waves*? I am a little clouded with headache.

It is our own fault – our diaries, of course. And not to have burned letters. Better not written them at all? Will they never cease, I wonder, this picking & pecking? This Bloomsberrying is, as Leonard says, sheer fudge.

If we could answer. But at least they cannot follow us here to turn out our cupboards in search of their cobweb gossip. And such a pleasure that we may visit. Leonard, you, Clive, Roger, Lytton, poor Carrington – even Ottoline (though not too often).

Lord! Nessa, do come! And let us have a burning of those books!!! Adders' tails & viper's gall, say I. Sheer fudge, says L.

    Do come –

        (Bring fish – I am nervous of dress-shops.)
        Yr.
        V.

THE BLOOMSBURY SET BOOK FACTORY

MICHAEL GREEN

Captain Horation Ramage
by Dudley O'Forester

I have invented this title to stand for a whole flood of eighteenth-century naval stories. I make no apology, since they are all the same anyway. I know, I've read them all and I'm still looking for one which is different. My greatest complaint is the unending courage shown. Every single person on the British side seems impervious to fear except for the Ship's Coward, and these are strictly rationed and inevitably slain hideously. We know the outcome of every battle before it starts since no ship commanded by the hero can be defeated except by Act of God or overwhelming odds. The enemy seem composed of buffoons and cretins unable to hit a British frigate from thirty yards.

The authors' obsession with victory drives them to extravagant lengths and Patrick O'Brien, his hero pursued by a much stronger Dutch ship, actually has the cheek to make the enemy sink suddenly after being overwhelmed by a freak wave. It is all rather the nautical equivalent of "with one bound Jack was free", and one is tempted to remind the authors that French children are taught to look upon Trafalgar as an indecisive naval engagement in which the British commander was killed.

When they run out of victories at sea, the gallant captains often seek it ashore, usually an absurd raid on a heavily defended fort with a handful of sailors and marines. They then return to a grateful Admiralty ("By God Hornblower/Ramage/Bolitho/Aubrey, old Boney would have a fit if he knew we had this information you gathered . . .")

All this is padded out to twice its proper length with incomprehensible although doubtless genuine period detail about putting up double preventer backstays and setting royal stuns'ls.

My greatest literary ambition is to see the mask slip and to read a book of this breed containing a passage like this: "Hornblower realised he had made a mistake in bracing up the lee clewsails. The French ship was forereaching fast and would soon catch them up. Retreat was impossible.

" 'Stand by to repel boarders!' Hornblower shouted. Nobody moved. His first lieutenant, Bush, was vomiting with fear over the side, his face green. Brown, his coxswain, was hunched trembling under a cannon with his hands firmly pressed over his ears. Most of the crew had hidden themselves below when the French approached.

" 'Damn you, will nobody go?' shouted Hornblower. 'Yes, if you'll lead us cap'n' called out an old seaman. That was just what Hornblower did not want. 'Lieutenant Bush will lead you, men' he called out desperately. 'My post is at the stern' ('Yes' he thought to himself, 'where I can strike the colours after a token resistance.') At the sound of his name Bush heaved himself upright and fled down a hatchway below. It was at that moment the French ship clawed alongside and hurled grappling irons. With a squeak of fright Hornblower jumped over the side . . ."

ALEX HAMILTON
Enriching Diet

I couldn't burn books, but I do recall that at one time there was a woman with a shop in Pimlico who was making furniture out of them, either because at that period books were cheaper than wood, or as her contribution to Save the Tree, and my candidate for conversion into occasional tables, with the jackets into lampshades and the promotional material into trampolines, is the Scarsdale Diet. About twenty years ago this was no more than an innocuous-looking sheet of paper passed around among fat friends who took private advice from Dr Herman Tarnower at the Scarsdale Medical Centre in New York. But the Ur-Diet was supplemented by tissue clones called Keep Trim Diet, Vegetarian Diet, the Gourmet Diet, the International Diet and the Money Saver Diet which, being pumped full of an oedema called creative publishing, swelled into a mighty concordance, made up of threats, boasts and exhortations, plus ecstatic references to jumbo olives and alcohol-free cocktails. The final title, like the rattle of a bag of bones, is *The Complete Scarsdale Medical Diet Plus Dr Tarnower's Lifetime Keep-Slim Program,* by Herman Tarnower, M.D. and Samm Sinclair Baker.

Since Dr Tarnower was shot dead in a bedroom skirmish with a discarded paramour and alleged contributor to the book, the headmistress of a pukka girls' school in Virginia, the book has sold a million copies in a year. We must however exonerate him on the charge of getting himself killed as a publicity stunt, as the thing had already sold three million before the distraught pedagogue pulled the trigger. But she was only one of many well-heeled, and round-heeled, women who looked for proof of the pudding in his bed, and one may ask if he was quite the avatar of moderation that his book projects. His abrupt end is doubly unfortunate in that now we can never know if he would otherwise have lived for ever on the strict régimes he recommended.

Dr Tarnower may have meant well. He has bulked out his book with testimonials from anonymous beneficiaries of the process – thus incidentally inventing a new kind of book which ingests its own hype. He is generous with steak, club soda and mountains of salad, and their merchandisers will salute him. He helps the fat idiot become a thin idiot by regular repetition of whole pages of the same advice. But the result can only encourage obsessionals to be even more boring about their weight.

"It is the lean, strong, well-tailored person who is admired today," declares the author roundly. Very, very few of the persons I have most admired fit this description. While I'd not go so far as to suggest the Burmese flattery, "You're looking very fat today," as an ideal courtesy for the Western world, I'd be saddened if zoftig and casual persons all melted away from society.

And "dieted", by the way, is an anagram of "edited". The makers of this puffball have either forgotten or, worse, cynically reversed, the magic in their own code.

Herman Tarnower and Samm Sinclair Baker, The Scarsdale Medical Diet *(first published 1980), Bantam, 1980*

TIM HEALD

Missing Persons

My edition of *Who's Who*, the 1980, has no Wedgie Benn, no Bernard Levin, not even, heaven help us, Ronald Reagan. (Is being a movie star, Governor of California and Republican candidate not enough? What else d'you have to do – become President of the United States? Yes, he's in the 1981 edition, as large as life.) The Secretary of the Department of Capital and Territory, Australia is in, so is the Overseas Labour Adviser at the Foreign and Commonwealth Office and the man who was once Physician-in-Charge of the X-Ray Department at St Thomas's Hospital. Any old headmaster of any two-bit minor public school gets a place as do the obscurest modern major-generals and some extraordinarily dim civil servants. Brian Clough doesn't; nor Geoffrey Boycott; nor Cilla Black.

Who's Who, indeed! Who says? And the rot doesn't stop there. Not only are half the people who are who left out and a lot of nonentities put in their place, but people write their own entries. This leads to all manner of self-indulgence. Some MPs leave their private addresses out as well as their phone numbers. So does Rupert Murdoch, whose desire for privacy means that he only gets eight lines whereas Sir John Fletcher-Cooke is allowed to have his membership of the Constituencies Delimitation Commn for Kenya 1962 in his boring entry which runs to more than fifty lines. And those dreadful whimsical "recreations": the professor of psychology who lists "do-it-yourself-house renovation", the octogenarian journalist who likes "taking the Left Wing intelligentsia at its own valuation"; the teacher who likes "brooding", the major-general who simply lists "numerous". Don't they employ editors at A. and C. Black?

It wouldn't matter if the book was merely a piece of

self-indulgent whimsy, but it's not. It is allegedly the only thing of its kind and as such it is an essential reference book for anyone interested in the world about us. No working journalist can do without it and yet no working journalist worth his salt can even begin to rely on it.

Who's Who *(first published 1849), Black, 1980*

ROBERT HELLER

Because of the Mints

The problem with really bad books is that only a masochist would actually read them, and I'm not given to masochistic exercises. There are books, like Mario Puzo's *The Godfather*, which are manifestly awful, but belong to a genre where literary incompetence and disgusting subject matter are no barrier to success. To qualify as a truly bad book, the work must have pretensions towards high quality. Better still, it should be widely applauded by ladies and gentlemen of taste. With this criterion in mind, I have no hesitation in nominating *La Comédie Humaine*, that sprawling collection of novels by Balzac.

My children, confusing my veneration for Zola with a non-existent admiration for Balzac, bought me several presents of the latter's work. Paternal feelings led me to read enough of them to confirm that they are pompous, far-fetched, given to tedious detail and impossible monologues, unconvincing psychologically, overblown dramatically, devoid of lyricism and not even containing a good yarn. How such piddling works contributed to the creation of so towering a figure in the French literary Pantheon escapes me completely. Perhaps it has something to do with the fascination Balzac had with financial investments, a trait that no doubt appeals to the French instinct for interest-bearing securities.

But even if Balzac's stories were based on something more credible than, for example, a piece of wild ass's skin that confers magical powers on its possessor, their appeal for me would be utterly destroyed by his habit of breaking off the narrative for the purpose of long and boring digressions. Of that, if nothing else, Balzac is the true master.

I have sought in vain for qualities that would better explain to me why Balzac is held in such high esteem.

But he doesn't even possess the genius for portraying character and evoking sentiment (or sentimentality) displayed by Charles Dickens, another master of padding and digression. Of course, to a true Dickensian, the padding and the word-spinning are part of the irresistible charm they find in the great Victorian novelist. Possibly, the same is true of lovers of Balzac. It seems to me the equivalent of going to a bad restaurant because you like the mints they serve with the coffee.

But the greatest condemnation of Balzac is that, in contrast to those of the other and far greater French novelists, such as Proust, Zola, Flaubert and de Maupassant, his characters are not real, living, human beings. They are literary devices used in the cause of a fundamentally non-literary obsession with incident and detail.

Mario Puzo, The Godfather *(first published in the UK, 1969), Pan, 1971*
Honoré de Balzac, La Comédie Humaine. *This consists of ninety novels and stories, including* Old Goriot *(first published 1835), Penguin, 1969 and* Cousin Bette *(first published 1846), Penguin, 1965*

BEVIS HILLIER

An Unfunny Thing Happened to Me

I once thought of writing a huge book called *The Anatomy of Hilarity* (or *Humour is a Funny Thing*). In it I would analyse what it is that makes people laugh. I soon realised this was a task almost as impossible as to analyse what it is that makes people fall in love with each other. I noted E. B. White's deterrent remark: "Humour can be dissected, as a frog can, but the thing dies in the process." But what really convinced me not to attempt the book, was reading *The Diary of a Nobody*.

Here was a book which rocked most of my friends in the aisles. Sir John Betjeman, whose sense of humour otherwise coincides with mine at all points, thinks it the funniest book ever written. I can truthfully say that I read it from cover to cover without the ghost of the shadow of a smile, let alone the uncurbable guffaws it seems to provoke in everybody else. (Though – to salvage my claim to a sense of humour – Dickens, Wodehouse and Waugh make me laugh out loud continually.)

The *Diary* first appeared in *Punch*, and the humour is of the kind which takes amusement in dropped aitches and the social gaffes of the Lower Orders. In fact, the book is one long sneer from beginning to end. We are invited to laugh at a lower-middle-class man who chooses the wrong paint for his staircase or the wrong wine for a party, and who wears a clip-on bow tie, the wretched snivelling creature. The odd sneer is aimed at the working class too ("Couldn't find umbrella . . . Sarah said Mr Gowing must have took it by mistake last night, as there was a stick in the 'all that didn't belong to nobody.") Most of the humour is on the level of feeble slapstick: every chapter is a chapter of accidents. And every joke is done to death after being worried like a bone by a dog. Take the affair of the door-scraper. Here are the successive stages of this tedious drama:

April 3   Cummings . . . fell over the scraper as he went out. Must get the scraper removed, or else I shall get into a *scrape*.

April 7   The Curate . . . caught his foot in the scraper, and tore the bottom of his trousers.

April 9   It was the blackguard butcher again, who said he had cut his foot over the scraper, and would immediately bring an action against me. Called at Farmerson's, the ironmonger, on my way to town, and gave him the job of removing the scraper . . .

April 10   Farmerson came round to attend to the scraper himself . . . He says he does not usually conduct such small jobs personally, but for me he would do so.

April 12   Left Farmerson repairing the scraper, but when I came home found three men working. I asked the meaning of it, and Farmerson said that in making a fresh hole he had penetrated the gas-pipe.

May 7   (Meeting Farmerson at the Lord Mayor's Ball) To think that a man who made our scraper should know any member of the aristocracy!

Well, some of you are probably in fits by now, but I still can't *scrape* up a smile, ho ho ho.

The humour of the *Diary* is derived ultimately from The Pickwick Papers; even the characters' names are Dickensian – Mr Pooter, Mr Perkupp, Sir William Grime. Dickens's genius created a transcendental facetiousness, jetting out like champagne from a shaken bottle. By contrast, the *Diary* is flat ginger beer. One might describe the humour as "laboured" if one felt that any effort at all had gone into it.

George and Weedon Grossmith, Diary of a Nobody (*first published 1894*), Penguin, 1965

MICHAEL HOLROYD
The Sound of Bubbles

I set my curse on *Swallows and Amazons*. This book blighted my childhood. My dominant feeling while growing up was that I didn't know what was going on. Even now I sometimes wonder. What *is* going on? I'm still not Shaw.

Thirty years of careful detective work has traced this feeling back to Arthur Ransome's inimitable – I hope inimitable — series of classics. They *were* classics. Everyone knew that. My grandfather knew it and so did my aunt. At any moment of crisis (Christmas, for instance, or my birthday) they would conjure up another of these volumes and smilingly hand it to me. And Ransome kept them coming too. He was an institution. *Swallows and Amazons*, the first of the series involving all those inscrutably sailing children, was published in 1930. Not until 1947 did he let up in Britain or America – except, significantly, for 1935, the year in which I was born.

I was born between *Coot Club* and *Pigeon Post*: and in due course I received them both. *But what were they about?* I couldn't make it out. Despite the almost indistinguishable jackets, my grandfather and my aunt took the trouble never to give me the same book twice. This was remarkable since they had never peeped inside any of them. I have since suspected that all bestsellers are made this way.

Out of politeness rather than human curiosity I would open *Swallows and Amazons* and struggle with a few pages as if writhing in *Finnegans Wake*. First there were the complicated endpapers, essential (so I understood) to a proper comprehension of the water-plot, showing maps heavily marked with boat houses, lagoons, bays, islands, reefs and rivers worming across the page into the sea. There were other maps too (with more rivers, bays, seas) among the illustrations. These were drawn by Ransome himself who liked to include portraits of boats with names such as *Teasal* and *Titmouse*, and to glory in their booms, jibs, keels, flags, foredecks, halyards and so on. Letting go these halyards, striking these flags, setting compasses, weighing anchors, booming, keeling, jibbing was what went on in these books. The children were continually doing such things and continually talking about doing them. I could visualise none of it. What did we know of tillers, topsails, telescopes at Maidenhead where I was quartered with my grandparents? I was apprehensive even of the pond at the bottom of the garden. Arthur Ransome was often praised for his verisimilitude, but for me all that sea-talk was no more than the sound of bubbles. In short: he had the bad manners to write as if I and my aunt did not exist.

It seems to me now that Arthur Ransome must have been a fascinating man. He was a literary critic, the biographer of Oscar Wilde, an expert on Russian folklore, perhaps a spy, certainly a war correspondent and widely-travelled *Manchester Guardian* journalist. But the books he wrote during his second childhood in the Lake District were for years a polite torture to me. I sank under them. Ever since then I have pondered such revenges – what they were yet I knew not, until invited to contribute to this book. Arthur Ransome didn't teach me language, but I know how to curse.

Arthur Ransome, Swallows and Amazons *(first published 1930), Puffin, 1970*
Swallowdale *(first published 1931)*
Peter Duck *(first published 1932), Puffin, 1968*
Winter Holiday *(first published 1933), Puffin, 1968*
Coot Club *(first published 1934), Puffin, 1969*
Pigeon Post *(first published 1936), Puffin, 1969*
We Didn't Mean to Go to Sea *(first published 1937), Puffin, 1969*
Secret Water *(first published 1939)*
The Big Six *(first published 1940), Puffin, 1970*
Missee Lee *(first published 1941), Puffin, 1971*
The Picts and the Martyrs *(first published 1943), Puffin, 1971*
Great Northern? *(first published 1947), Puffin, 1971*

ROLAND HUNTFORD
Little Árpád

If there is a book against which I feel personal resentment, it is Freud's *Totem and Taboo*. It destroyed my adolescence.

One rainy afternoon in the school holidays, I noticed the work nestling on a handy bookshelf: a slim blue and white Penguin (or was it a Pelican?) exposed to anybody's inspection, regardless of age and condition. *Totem and Taboo*; what a splendid title, what titillating undertones did it not suggest? I dipped into the volume. Having been nurtured on Christopher Robin, I suddenly found myself up against Little Árpád.

Little Árpád, for those who have forgotten, is a star – *the* star? – of *Totem and Taboo*. He was a young Hungarian who, on his summer hols, at the age of two-and-a-half, "tried to urinate into the chicken-run", as Freud put it, "and a fowl had bitten or snapped at his penis." Which had the makings of a jolly good limerick. Unfortunately, I did not "lisp in numbers". Even more unfortunately, I read on.

It seems that because of the fowl's attention, Little Árpád "formed his own choice of sexual objects on the model of life in the chicken-run, for he said one day to the neighbour's wife: 'I'll marry you and your sister and my three cousins and the cook; no, not the cook. I'll marry my mother instead.'" So that, Freud declared, "Little Árpád's poultry perversion was a product of the Oedipus complex." From that, by a progression of dicta guaranteed to impress a thirteen-year-old, he informed me, the reader, that, "The beginnings of religion, morals, society and art converge in the Oedipus complex."

So, just as faith and love were beginning to stir, I was pitchforked into religion and sex. When I should have been treading the long, deceptive path to bed, I took the soft option and cantered round the psychoanalyst's couch. Instead of mooning round some local goddess – or even falling in love with some Hollywood Aphrodite – I was considering "little Árpád's poultry perversion". Psychoanalysis was all.

Having become a juvenile Freudian, I naturally saw sex behind everything. I must needs hold forth on Oedipus and all that. It was enough – quite rightly – to scare off any decent girl willing to help even so awkward a specimen as myself over the sacred threshold.

So my growing up was festooned by Little Árpád, his close connection Little Hans, and all the other "cases" presented by Freud. It took me a long time to discover that Freud was simply trying to explain Viennese jokes. It was a pity, for the man was undeniably an artist. What plots could he not have contrived for the theatre and the opera house; what librettos for Hindemith and Strauss. Instead of which, he had squandered his talent on Little Árpád. Freud suddenly seemed a Viennese joke himself. The guru had dissolved. The scales had fallen from my eyes.

But by then it was too late. *Totem and Taboo* had deprived me of my youth. Freud has a lot to answer for.

Sigmund Freud, Totem and Taboo *(first published 1913),*
Routledge 1950

BRIAN INGLIS

Cradle and All

In a recent public opinion poll taken in the United States, Sir James Frazer's *The Golden Bough* came out high among the top twenty "most influential books" in history. I imagine it would probably get a similar ranking in Britain. Yet its proper place is among the top twenty literary/scientific confidence tricks.

Frazer did no anthropological field-work. What he did was work his way through the mass of material coming in during the nineteenth century from explorers, missionaries and the like, fuse it in with historical accounts, and then supply his own synthesis. Unluckily the synthesising process took over early in the proceedings, compelling him to disregard whatever evidence did not fit, and to distort the rest to make it fit.

The first volumes of *The Golden Bough*, published in 1890, created an enormous impression by virtue of what appeared to be their author's erudition. It was not until 1899 that Mary Kingsley, returning from her travels in Africa, described how she had brought it with her as Bible and *vade mecum*, only to find that it bore no resemblance to reality.

Why, then, had anthropologists allowed themselves to be deceived? The reason was that the more gifted of them, men like Tylor and Marett, had not been deceived; but anthropology at that time was in so delicate a situation academically – Tylor had only just occupied the first professorial Chair, at Oxford – that they did not care to foul their doorstep.

It was left to Andrew Lang, in 1902, to eviscerate *The Golden Bough* in *Magic and Religion*, revealing just how spurious Frazer's method had been. But Lang, though a polymath of genius, was not an anthropologist; and Frazer could afford to ignore him. Between 1912 and 1915 twelve volumes of the grotesquely overblown third edition appeared; in 1914 Frazer received his knighthood; and in 1925, his OM.

No anthropologist now takes Frazer seriously; but nobody since Lang has attempted the daunting task of demolishing *The Golden Bough*, step by step, for the benefit of the public. As a result it is still widely regarded as a classic; many people, in fact, acquire their initial knowledge, and some their only knowledge, of anthropology from the abridged paperback version.

And Frazer has more to answer for, because a stream of similarly bogus works were churned up in *The Golden Bough's* wake. The most notorious was Margaret Murray's *The Witch-cult in Western Europe*, the book chiefly responsible for the current public image of witches. As Professor Norman Cohn has pointed out, her ideas were "firmly set in an exaggerated and distorted version of the Frazerian mould". The book is simply rubbish; yet it, too, retains public esteem.

Frazer must surely also bear some of the responsibility for the development for that curse of our times, Structuralism. Anthropologists needed a structure to replace the ruins of golden-boughery; Lévi-Strauss provided one for them. As a result, much of present-day anthropology is childish – as well as unreadable, because of the excruciating jargon.

James Frazer, The Golden Bough *(first published 1890), abridged edition, Macmillan Paperbacks, 1980*
Andrew Lang, Magic and Religion *(first published 1902), Greenwood Press*
Margaret Murray, The Witch-Cult in Western Europe, *Clarendon Press, 1921*

DAVID IRVING
The X + 1 Phenomenon

I'm sometimes asked what I would do if I discovered that an author of far greater repute was about to complete a manuscript on the same subject as mine. (You'd be surprised how often it happens. Somehow the word gets around, and in no time at all there are two or three authors panting down the same paths and knocking on the same front doors.)

I'm going to keep it to myself, but I've now worked out a plan: in fact it's one of the most fiendish tricks I could devise, a dead cert to ruin the rival's chances of beating me to the post. I shall wait until he's within two or three weeks of mailing his finished typescript to his publishers, and then I'm going to Xerox my entire research files – linear-yards of the stuff – parcel them up in studied disorganisation, and mail them to him with a note of fulsome capitulation. "Your own work," I shall write, "is bound to be so infinitely superior to my own, nay it will clearly become the standard work in libraries and learning establishments throughout the world; what selfish right have I to use my modest researches exclusively in my own far more modest volume? Here! – Take all my files!"

This Danaic gift, or so I speculate, will hit my rival right in his literary midriff. He knows that he will ignore these thousands of new pages at his peril. So he will be dazzled by them, he will struggle to incorporate them, his pagination will go to pot, and he will end up submitting his manuscript late, muddled and disjointed beyond recognition.

Alas! I hit on this ploy too late to prevent Joachim Fest's footlocker of a biography of Adolf Hitler from reaching the bookstands in 1974, six months before my own. It is stylistically perfect, but penned with the supreme innocence of the biographer who once told a questioner that he had not even visited the magnificent National Archives in Washington which houses by far the largest collection of records relating to recent European history. It is the laboratory specimen of what I term the $x + 1$ phenomenon: a biographer buys x books on his chosen subject, and writes the $x + 1th$. Fest has, in my view, swallowed uncritically questionable documents, faked diaries and concocted memoirs printed by the apologians of defeat after the war. His book will pollute historiography for generations.

This magician of the pen has conjured up old legends and gilded them like new. In the good old days sorcerers like Fest were burnt at the stake; in recent, less enlightened, years, their books were tossed on the pyre instead. If ever a book deserved consigning to the unforgiving flames, it is Fest's *Hitler*: unoriginal, turgid, erratic, prosaic – swallowed by millions of German readers, digested by few of them.

I am deeply conscious of my own share of the guilt.

If only I had hit on my ploy sooner. "Dear Joachim," I would have written as I parcelled up my files, "aware as I am, in all humility, of my own inadequacy . . ."

Joachim C. Fest, Hitler *(first published 1974), Penguin, 1977*

D.A.N. JONES
Bitter Plums

George Orwell was a likeable writer. He blends basic leftism ("Always support the poor against the rich") with patriotism so smoothly that sentimental readers do not always notice how close he is to National Socialism, how near his voice to Hitler's.

Take *The Lion and the Unicorn*, published in 1941, in which he comes out with one of his celebrated epigrams: "England is a family with the wrong members in control." The third section of the book, "The English Revolution" describes his ideal of a post-war government.

"It will have nationalised industry, scaled down incomes, set up a classless educational system . . . It will shoot traitors but it will give them a solemn trial beforehand, and occasionally acquit them. It will crush any open revolt promptly and cruelly . . ."

Why nationalisation? "Socialism," he claims, "unlike capitalism, can solve the problems of production and consumption . . . In a socialist economy these problems do not exist. The state simply calculates what goods will be needed and does its best to produce them . . ."

Education? "We could start by abolishing the autonomy of the public schools and the older universities . . . There is a danger that some of the older schools will survive as festering centres of snobbery . . ."

The Empire? "No need for the British to protect the worthless life of the [Indian] moneylender, to prefer the half-barbarous Gurkha to the educated Bengali . . ."

What is needed is "new blood, new men, new ideas – in the true sense of the word, a revolution . . . It is very necessary that industry should be nationalised, but it is more urgently necessary that such monstrosities as butlers and 'private incomes' should disappear forthwith . . . The working classes will have to suffer terrible things. They will want some kind of proof that a better life is ahead . . . The one sure earnest of that is that when they are taxed and overworked they shall see that the rich are being hit even harder. And if the rich squeal audibly, so much the better . . . The lady in the Rolls-Royce car is more damaging to morale than a fleet of Göring's bombing-planes . . . There will be a bitter political struggle. At some point or other it may be necessary to use violence . . ."

It will be said that I have taken these quotations "out of context". I say that I have pulled these bitter plums from the syrup. Read them aloud, in a high, hysterical, Hitlerian voice and see how you like them.

George Orwell, The Lion and the Unicorn *(first published 1941), Secker and Warburg, 1962*

H. R. F. KEATING

Dagger in the Back

Crime fiction is almost always reviewed in a manner rather different from the treatment meted out to its mainstream aunt. It gets it easier. Ocean-depth silence is the unkindest cut allowed to the crime critic.

But let us take an example of current crime fiction and for once allot it the sort of attention it might get were it worth taking only half seriously. We must choose a book hailed to a reasonable extent by these crime critics as an example of their art, and we must choose one that has succeeded by something more than the pecuniary test of public acceptance, a test that can be manoeuvred by the wizards of the hype process right down to convincing readers they liked a book they merely contrived to finish.

Happily for our purposes the principal crime reviewers meet annually under the auspices of the Crime Writers Association to decide in solemn, and slightly bibulous, conclave what book shall be awarded a Golden Dagger. Yet perhaps we should also go back in time enough to select for our rather more rigorous than usual examination a volume for which the years have confirmed in some way or another the lunch-time verdict of the pundits of its year.

So let us choose the 1964 winner of the award, a book that introduced a "new detective" who in subsequent volumes attained his place on the puny tree of historical criticism of the genre. And let us begin by looking at the people portrayed, since depiction of character is perhaps the root and key of the business of novel-making.

What do we find? At first glance: energy. Fireworks, you might say. But beyond the splutter and incandescence? Stock. Samples taken from that big, old cupboard, dusted down, patted, shaken and inserted *ad libitum*. The most notable character, for example, is a businessman who prevents the detective from getting on with the business of solving the crime. Oh, what a character, we exclaim unthinkingly. (It is in an unthinking state that such books as these are read.) Yet look more closely and what do we see? The stage fat man, villainous version. Plenty of swinging contradictions, but they are contradictions of rhetoric rather than the genuine contradictions of personality. Easy characterisation, and it accompanies other easy pickings scattered piecemeal through the pages. Easy pathos: the victim (he never actually dies: smart piece of showy contrivance) is seen lying unconscious. "Three ballpoint pens were neatly clipped on to one of his pockets. The red one had leaked and a small pinkish stain . . ." Easy. Easy jokes: there is a Minister involved, and what portfolio does he hold? You could probably guess, given a minute. Yes. Minister for Police Affairs and the Arts. Easy, easy.

And the actual writing? Again, at first glance: energy. Fizz even. But I do not wish to praise with faint damns. Look harder. Tricks abound. Easy old echoes. One of the suspects is found, suspiciously, reading a book with, wait for it, a "lurid cover on which a square-jawed private eye was for ever menacing a busty blonde." Keats, thou shouldst be with us . . .

But who is with us? Only Keating. And what does he tag along with him? Not the perfection of a Grecian urn, but the sad imperfections of *The Perfect Murder*. I wish it had been something very different.

H. R. F. Keating, The Perfect Murder, *Collins, 1964*

MILES KINGTON
Her Arms Akimbo

I was once told by an interpreter from the European
Parliament that the hardest speeches of all to translate
simultaneously were those read word for word from a
prepared draft. When politicians spoke off the cuff, and
gesticulated and acted, you could follow the natural
rhythms of their speech; but the fully prepared oration
came across flat and lifeless, and very hard to turn into
another language, even though the sense itself was clear
enough.

I know the feeling. I once had to read *King Arthur and
the Knights of the Round Table* by Antonia Fraser out
loud to my children. It is probably the only book ever
written in the same kind of language as speeches in the
European Parliament; certainly, it is the only book I
have read out loud to my children which necessitated
rephrasing almost every sentence as I went along, for
the simple reason that otherwise they found it difficult to
know what on earth it was all about. The language is not
exactly the same, of course; where a Euro-MP would
talk about tariff controls or national aspirations or
fishing limits, Lady Antonia talks about swoons and
gritted teeth and people's blood boiling and vowing to
tame the proud beauty, but the numbing effect is the
same.

As Arthurian characters cannot talk like MPs, some
experimenting is needed for the dialogue, which is based
on several different models (public-school novels, bad
old historical movies, women's magazine stories of the
worst sort), all of which share one thing in common: that
nobody talks like that. Examples: —

"I feel tremendously excited at the thought of this
adventure," says Gareth.

I don't believe anyone ever said that.

"Is your father in the castle?" says Merlin to Arthur
and Kay.

Nothing wrong with that. Except that it isn't quite what Merlin says. What he says in the book is, " 'Is your father, Sir Hector, in the castle?' " Just in case Arthur and Kay had forgotten what their father's name was? To remind the reader? To remind the author?

The two boys replied that he was somewhere about his estates. I find that hard to believe as well. I have often asked children where their father was, but not a single one has ever said to me: He is somewhere about his estates.

(Asked whether he yielded) . . . " 'I have no alternative,' replied the knight between gritted teeth. 'But I shall have my revenge one day, Geraint of Devon, on you and your bride.' " Note the gritted teeth. Note that he did not give in, or surrender, but *yielded*. And note that the knight calls him Geraint of Devon face to face, so that Geraint shall not forget his own name, or indeed the part of England that he comes from. And what do you think Geraint of Devon did in reply? Yes, of course: he "dismissed his threats with a laugh".

This constant anxiety that the reader should know who exactly is talking to whom, and what plans of revenge are being hatched, is best exemplified in this passage: —

"Little did the conspirators know that their talks have been overheard by an unseen witness . . . 'Morgan le Fay suspects something,' Merlin said aloud; 'I did not think that her spells were strong enough to get so near the truth. But just now I read in her mind uneasy thoughts about the old prophecy . . .' "

The chief feature of that little episode, apart from the confusing nature of the cross-suspecting, is the first appearance in fiction, so far as I know, of the character who can not only read people's minds but also has to speak aloud to find out what he has just read in their minds.

Here are three more passages for you to mull over. To help, I have appended a few useful questions.

1 "He ordered the heralds to blow their trumpets from the battlements. It was war! A week later, with head held high, Arthur rode out from Camelot on a magnificent

white horse at the head of his men."

(Why do you think it took a week between the announcement of war, and their riding forth? Does it take a week to find a good enough white horse? Or to get your head up high enough? Or had it simply just taken seven days for the heralds to recover the trumpets they had so unfortunately blown from the battlements?)

2 " 'Let me be!' she cried in Spanish.
'Do not fear,' replied Tristram."

(Given that up to this point in the story Tristram has only talked Cornish, how do you account for his miraculous ability to have a conversation in Spanish? Do you think there is a missing week, not mentioned, in which he took Spanish lessons?)

3 " 'That is the strangest sight in the world!' exclaimed Arthur to Merlin. Four ox-carts were struggling up the road, weighed down by an enormous burden. 'A Round Table,' continued the king. 'Yes, it's a huge Round Table!' "

(Do you think you would be able to recognise a round table immediately? Especially if it was on four ox-carts and therefore presumably divided into four pieces? With the legs probably coming on afterwards? And how did Arthur know it was a Round Table, not a round table?)

But giving little extracts from this book can hardly convey the full flavour of the entire work, which among other things has an entirely new style of sports reporting. Lady Antonia, I would guess, has little interest in the technical side of fencing and jousting, which enables her to write summaries like this: —

"Against five knights, Geraint managed to hold his own, and distribute blows which crippled his opponents. Two knights fell to the ground, mortally wounded; then a third; then a fourth; finally only Agravaine himself remained. Geraint summoned all his failing strength and pierced the evil man through and through."

Or, in modern terms . . . Arsenal eventually scored one goal; then later they scored another; at the final whistle they had won two-nil, but all the team felt very tired.

I can only urge you to look out the book yourself,

which I believe is unique. And if you do, take a look at page 103. There you will find the girl who cried "Let me be" in Spanish. But she had done this "folding her arms akimbo". Now, given that akimbo means with hands on hips and elbows spread out, try to explain how this can be done with your arms folded.

Antonia Fraser, King Arthur and the Knights of the Round Table *(first published 1954), re-issued by Sidgwick and Jackson, 1970*

PAUL LEVY
Cooking: The Books

Ordinarily, the only reason for which I should counten-
ance banning books is that they bore me. On that
ground I should quite happily agree to there being no
more books *about* Virginia Woolf or by Martin Amis.

Still, I should like to see at least a moratorium on the
writing and publishing of cookery books. (I don't like the
American term, "cook book".) Cookery books are very
seldom boring. What they more often are is sick-
making.

Any book advocating short-cuts in the kitchen is
bound to have at least one nausea-inducing chapter on
the use of tinned mushroom soup in casseroled dishes of
unthinkable nastiness. Most of these books – and there
are many of them – are written by and for housewives
who imagine they are not only good cooks but the
possessors of extraordinary culinary secrets that would
give a fillip to the spatula of Escoffier himself.

In fact they are poisoners, who get away with their
crimes because their husbands are cowards and their
children have had their taste-buds corrupted by the
junk-food industry and their palates raped by school
dinners. The situation in America is even worse; the
Japanese are, by all accounts, succumbing to junk-food
imperialism; France fell long ago.

Examples are not hard to come by. A recent book,
now in its second printing, carries a recipe for soup made
from, among other things, dried onions, a large packet
of Smash and tinned carrots. Admitted, the author has a
sense of humour, as she calls it "soup *Mauvaise Femme*"
and signs herself Lucrezia; but she does claim that it can
be eaten.

Other horrors that crossed my desk in the last year
included a noisome recipe for packeted frankfurters in
tinned tomato sauce, which is recommended for
slimmers. I'm sure it would work, as even the cat would

throw up if it ate the food shown in the colour illustration the foolish publishers paid a fortune to print opposite page 250 of this unfortunate book.

A special hate of mine is worthy cookery books. These take more than one form. Sometimes they are slight tomes praising the diet of manioc and chilli peppers that is the exclusive nourishment of some third-world country. More often they are straightforward vegetarian tracts, extolling the virtues of fart food, printed on thick beige paper, with photographs of dishes whose colour is basic bean brown.

The most egregious excess I know is the seemingly successful (many) part-work foisted upon the newsagent by one of our most distinguished cookery-book writers and restaurateurs. In an early number he had an equally well-known colleague writing about Chinese food.

Next to a recipe for untypical but delicious-sounding lamb stir-fried with leeks was a large, glossy, full-colour picture of the dish, served up, as it was cooked, in the wok. It is shown accompanied by one of those handsome split bamboo whisks that bears a close resemblance to a Western cooking tool. The Chinese, however, use it for scrubbing out the wok after it is used; to Chinese eyes, the photograph is the visual equivalent of using the washing-up brush to stir the *boeuf bourguignon*. And about as appetising.

GEORGE MACBETH

Without a Plot

I could dwell on the flaws in the *Bhagavad Gita* or Gurdjieff. I don't much like *Middlemarch* or *James Bond's Moonraker*, the book of the film. But perhaps the most disappointing of all unread works is the dictionary. Yes, the dictionary.

It comes in many forms, from the multi-volume O.E.D. to the pocket phrasebook, but you can count on the basic non-plot and non-impact always being the same: from aardvark to zymurgy we're offered one of the least emotive, and most illogical, reads in the language. Hands up anyone who's ever got through a single letter of it without skipping?

Nowadays the book often masquerades under a guise of anonymity, but the faults of the thing can be squarely laid at the door of its founding father, who – like God, in his day – wound up the little clockwork mechanism and then went off and forgot all about it. I mean, of course, Dr Johnson.

All subsequent editions bear the marks of this Leavisite old fraud's egotism. Literature ought to let you make up your own mind. Dictionaries lay down the law. It wouldn't be so bad if they took the trouble to weave a decent plot, or offer their principles through the mouths of rounded characters. They don't.

In fact, you very rarely find a proper name mentioned. As for settings and description, you can search in vain for any reference to a specific place. Everything happens in a dictionary in a kind of timeless void.

As for the style, it's ungrammatical and turgid – incomplete sentences, bad paragraphing, and over-fussy punctuation. Spelling? Yes, that's pretty good. But is it enough?

Here we have a large, very heavy and frequently expensive book, rivalling the Bible in popularity, but without a quarter of that old classic's action and colour. Where in the dictionary can you find anything to equal the scene where Abraham takes his son to sacrifice on the mountain?

Who would make large claims for the fourteen sections on "decision" in the Shorter Oxford? Or Webster's definition of "net"? These are minor flashes in the pan. If you really want a good flurry of associations, try the "Smith, L.J" section in the London Telephone Directory.

Even on its own ground the dictionary is outmoded and outclassed. For sheer bigotry, try the *Encyclopaedia Britannica*, and for better date references, *Who's Who in Baton Twirling*.

It's going to be an on-going bestseller, I know, but here's one reviewer who's giving a firm thumbs down to the dictionary in all its forms.

KENNETH McLEISH
Hem, Hem

A generation ago, to attack Hemingway in print would have been an act of literary suicide – and perhaps it still is. Many other writers have, in their day, been deified, but few can ever have evoked such unanimous and universal admiration. Hemingway is a "people's writer" (that is, enormously readable and popular), and he is a "writer's writer" (that is, outstanding at his craft). He tells exciting stories in fine, plain language, and appears also to pack them with a sustained philosophical commentary on the nature and predicament of man. At least two of his books — *Fiesta* and *A Farewell to Arms* — are ranking masterworks; perhaps *The Old Man and the Sea* (which occasioned his Nobel Prize) is one as well.

Hemingway's combination of greatness and accessibility is the root of the problem. His stature and his talent have led to a remarkably uncritical acceptance of what he has to say, of the view of man he proposes – and that view of man, in my opinion, is wholly vile. His books promote the idea of violence as a clean and cleansing force: to be a man, in Hemingway, you must be good with fists, rod, knife and gun. The natural kingdom exists to be hooked, impaled or shot – and the orgasmic satisfaction such slaughter produces in the hunter extends to warfare: one of the most serious charges against Hemingway is that he reduces the killing of other men (especially low-caste aliens such as spics, wops, dagoes and krauts) to a callous ritual about as moving (to the killer) as blowing his nose. It can be argued that Hemingway did not invent the culture of blood (or, for that matter, redneck literature), but merely reflected a prevalent morality. But his books (and their countless imitations in pulp fiction, films and on television) have promoted uncivilised brutality in western man to an extent unparalleled by any other creative artist. And if his men are brutes, his women are ciphers. Decorative or slatternly, they have no existence beyond the need to support their men – and the reason is that Hemingway men are almost without exception effeminate, achieving masculinity only by marrying themselves to such *macho* activities as hunting, boozing, warfare and the ruthless elimination of sentiment for anything but a noble piece of game or a game old buddy.

In Hemingway's best books, this ruthlessness is tempered by laconic wit, by superb descriptions of duck-shoots, shark-hunts and bull-fights, and – more rarely – by compassion for his characters: *A Farewell to Arms* even depicts a warm human relationship, on equal terms, between man and wife. But lesser Hemingway – it is the majority, and *To Have and Have Not* is typical — is a glum procession of grunts, gasps, gritted teeth and guts. Harry Morgan, the "hero" of *To Have and Have Not*, is the archetypal Hemingway "free spirit": a boozy, under-educated boor plying a leaky boat between the Florida Keys and Cuba, sometimes for dudes out fishing (whom he despises, patronises and wheedles), sometimes for gun-runners or revolutionaries (whom he fears, cheats and kills). His activities cost him, successively, his boat, his livelihood, his limbs and his life – he is literally cut down to size before our eyes – but the book's power lies less in its equivocal attitude to Morgan himself than in the gloatingly detailed and sickeningly brilliant descriptions of every fist-fight, knifing or shooting in which he is involved.

Kate Millett has written (in her book *Sexual Politics*) an impressive indictment of such other practitioners of *macho* literature as Miller and Mailer. Hemingway is a greater figure than any of her targets, and that's what makes him dangerous. Or is he (God forbid) right after all? Is the nightmare world of Harry Morgan and his like – a world which also embraces the protagonists of *Apocalypse Now, Death Race 2000* and *The Texas Chainsaw Massacre* — the real world after all? If it is, and Hemingway is thus a true prophet, then he has earned his eminence as much as the prophet Jeremiah earned his. But if it is not, if there is hope and decency still left in man, then the charges against Hemingway (of corrupt excellence, of dazzling falseness) are serious indeed.

Ernest Hemingway, Fiesta *(first published 1926), Panther, 1976*

A Farewell to Arms *(first published 1929), Panther, 1977*

The Old Man and the Sea *(first published 1952), Panther, 1976*

To Have and Have Not *(first published 1937), Panther, 1977*

Kate Millett, Sexual Politics *(first published in the UK, 1971), Virago, 1977*

FAY MASCHLER
Pretty Thin

I would say that it is possible to dislike a book on the grounds of finding the name of the author perfectly disagreeable. The very worst diet book I have read this week is written by Nathan Pritikin and Patrick McGrady. Itty. Bitty. Pritty. Prik. Thin. Thin will get you places. Thin is healthy. Everything you like to eat couldn't be worse for you.

Nathan has devised *The Pritikin Program for Diet and Exercise*. Note the spelling of the third word. The man, the book, is, of course, American. The Moral Majority who scooped Reagan into power have nothing on those who uphold the American ethic of dietary self-denial. Religion is one thing. You can also be puritanical (Pritikinical) about what you consume. The comparison is not casual. There are documented in the book, naturally, the case histories, the miracles.

Lazarus was raised from the dead. OK. Nate, in his own words, "outfoxed the Grim Reaper's cardiac division". Old Laz probably had good old dropsy, palsy, flopsy, or one of those Peter Rabbit diseases people used to die of. N.P. turned a corner signposted hypercholesterolemia, atherosclerosis, posterior wall myocardial ischaemia. Consider Eula Weaver. At about the age of eighty she had also spotted the GR on the horizon. After embarking on the Pritikin program she was able, in stages, to throw away her drugs, ride ten miles daily on her stationary bicycle, win ten gold medals in the National Senior Olympics and now at the age of ninety she jogs one mile daily, lifts weights twice weekly, and feels "as fit as a fiddle".

The fiddle, it seems to me, is that a life of pleasurable eating and drinking is constantly being decried in best-selling paperbacks as just the thing to do you down. And I buy the books. I sense that what they are saying is right.

But if, one day, God inspired an Angevin chef to reduce shallots, white wine vinegar and dry white wine and whisk in butter over a judiciously assessed heat so that it foamed and melted but did not separate, to make *beurre blanc*, surely we are supposed to eat it. Preferably with some turbot.

Old Pritikin rules out alcohol, coffee, tea, egg yolks, butter, oils, cheeses, nuts (except chestnuts), cream, caviar, offal, barbecued foods, duck, goose, bacon, sausages. An easy way to remember the rules is that if you like it, you mustn't have any. Also he instructs us to get up very early in the morning and go for a long walk. "Save the car for blizzards, floods, hurricanes, tornadoes and warfare"; all situations I would have thought when you might be better off on your own pins, or anyway tucked up in bed.

There are several reasons for disliking this and similar books. I know that if I passed my days eating buckwheat groats and shredded raw cabbage and skimmed milk I would live longer and probably look better, which chips away at a profound enjoyment of cooking and eating and supplies endless resolutions which I then feel badly about not sticking to. The books deny the civilising aspects of the meal-time and delicious food, a phenomenon that does well starting at home. They are obscene in the face of how, in other respects, life is conducted. Yoko Ono was reported as saying that she and Lennon pursued a careful diet with a view to living longer and more healthily. Since December she has said to Sean (their son) "Eat what you want."

Nathan Pritikin and Patrick McGrady, The Pritikin Program for Diet and Exercise *(first published 1979), Bantam, 1981*

SHERIDAN MORLEY
Not Good For You

I cannot remember precisely when I first began to loathe *The Guinness Book of Records*, though I would still wish here to claim the record for having loathed it longer and more deeply than any other reader or indeed any other book.

Originally, in my childhood, it seemed to be entirely full of out-of-focus snaps of daft Hungarian pole-vaulters doing themselves injuries; as it is now claiming to be twenty-seven and I am claiming to be forty (is this a record?) I must have been about thirteen, a deeply susceptible age at which to be brought face to face with the realisation that somebody had already jumped higher, dived deeper and run further than I was ever likely to manage.

Not that I ever wanted or intended to try, but it still irritated me that mere physical fitness and dexterity could be a claim to some sort of immortality in print. For several years thereafter, hopeful relatives eyeing an early pot-belly, mine rather than theirs, would solemnly present it to me for Christmas and for most of the 1950s I held the record for the largest number of consecutive unopened editions of *The Guinness Book of Records*.

Then, at some point in the 1960s, by which time I was mercifully too old and out of condition to be given it by any save the most eccentrically optimistic, something very bizarre happened. Instead of filling itself up with athletes and boxers and midgets and people of that ilk, it suddenly began to give space to contestants who could be sick into paper bags for more than a day. By the time I picked it up again in 1981 (for the purposes of this research) it had come to resemble nothing so much as a demented quiz show on day-time American television, in which entrants are for ever trying to outdo each other in pointless exercises of mind-numbing insanity.

Not only do I not care that Willie Hollingsworth of Freeport, New York holds the record for balancing a full pint of milk on his head for more than eighteen miles but

I deeply resent being told it, and object even more strongly to the number of trees that have been cut down in order to impart that totally useless knowledge to the world at large.

Being left alone with *The Guinness Book of Records* is like being trapped in a pub corner by some demented drunk who wishes to tell you things you have no desire or need to hear; moreover the things you do want to know aren't even there, viz the final score in the longest pinball game on record or whether this has now been overtaken by a player on Space Invaders.

Still more disconcerting is the shaky reliability of the whole ghastly publishing endeavour; not only is it highly questionable to give a "most durable actor" award to Richard Hearne merely because he began acting at six weeks and carried on till he was sixty-eight (think how many Victorian actors were carried on stage as babies and went on well into their eighties; consider indeed Lewis Casson who started at fourteen and was at it way past eighty-five) but it is actually wrong to announce that the smallest theatre in the world is on Mull when there's a gentleman in regular professional performance working from a canopied motorised tricycle to my certain knowledge. And if those two mistakes turn up on one single page, what can the rest of the facts be like?

What we need now is an entry for the most unnecessary book in the world.

The Guinness Book of Records (first published 1955 and thereafter annually), ed. N. D. McWhirter, Guinness Superlatives Ltd. 1981

THE RECORD FOR THROWING AWAY THE GUINNESS BOOK OF RECORDS

CHARLES OSBORNE
Backfired

Years ago, Brigid Brophy, Michael Levey, and I published a book called *Fifty Works of English Literature We Could Do Without*. The time has now come for me to admit that the work I really like least of all is one which I myself wrote. Its title is *Ned Kelly*; it was published by Anthony Blond in 1970, and it is the only book I have written which I would disown if I could. It came into existence because Anthony Blond, having learned that Mick Jagger was to star in a film based on the life of the Australian bushranger, asked me if I would be interested in writing a biography of Kelly which would be published on the day of the movie's premiere, would cash in on the expected success of the movie, and would earn large sums of money for us both.

My first impulse was to say, "No, Anthony, you've got the wrong kind of Australian. Why don't you ask Russell Braddon?" In fact, I seem to remember I did say this, but Anthony persisted and offered me a sufficiently large advance for my greed to vanquish my common sense. I ought to have known that Mick Jagger would be absolutely awful as Ned Kelly, but I did not know, until the day dawned when my book (written during a summer holiday at a friend's house in the south of France) was published, and the movie was released. I had to attend the premiere and when I was interviewed on TV later that evening and asked to comment on Mr Jagger's spiritual quality, common sense was vanquished this time by a rare attack of frankness. "Mick Jagger," I informed BBC viewers, "is about as spiritual as an Australian outdoor lavatory."

The film was, of course, a ghastly flop. Its American release was cancelled, and the American publishers who had paid me for the right to publish an edition in the United States hurriedly paid me even more to be freed of the obligation to publish.

The book, hastily cobbled together from nineteenth-century newspaper reports of the activities of Ned Kelly and his gang which a friend in Australia had sent to me, sold surprisingly well in Great Britain (and of course in Australia where books about Australia, however bad, always succeed), and even went into a paperback edition. However, when I was asked to revise and expand it for re-publication, I refused, for I was already feeling ashamed of having written it in the first place.

I had, however, taken the precaution of inserting secretly into the first edition of the book my real opinion of its hero, an opinion which, more than a decade later, I am prepared to reveal to the world. At the end of the book I had included a section of ballads and songs known to have been sung in Victoria during the lifetime of the Kelly Gang. One of these eight poems, a twelve-line fragment called *Stringybark*, is spurious. My opinion of Ned Kelly can be discovered by reading the initial letter of each line:

> Four of them rode away, that day,
> under a summer sky,
> carrying rifles on their backs.
> 'Kelly,' they said, 'must die.'
>
> Ned and his three mates kept alert,
> eager to join the fight.
> Dan, Joey Byrne and young Steve Hart
> knew all the police by sight.
>
> Evening it was, at Stringybark,
> light faded from the sky.
> Lonigan, drowsing by the fire,
> yawned, while the Gang passed by.

Charles Osborne, Ned Kelly *(first published 1970), Sphere, 1970*

JOHN OSBORNE
Grievous Bodily Harm

Vladimir Nabokov is surely the most preposterous Transylvanian monster ever to be created by American Academe. He is not a writer at all but a looming beast that stalks the Old Dark House of Campus Literature. Above all, he is what he himself would no doubt call, *dépassé*. Like a wounded laboratory artefact of some malign accident of European history, he lopes around his life and unreadable books, exploding with inexplicable monster's mirth at his own horrific destiny. Old Vladimir Karloff, stomping roguishly between St Petersburg, Russia, and St Petersburg, Florida, is set on a Hammer course of destruction, bashing his exile's club foot on anything around and the English language in particular.

One can see why his escape from the lab back there in downtown St Petersburg around 1917 has intimidated simple campus souls. He stands over his reader a little like a scowling *sommelier* waiting for his customers to let him make up their miserable uninstructed minds for them.

Nabokov gives literature a bad name apart from his overpowering inability to write. Reading a concerted passage from any of his works is like seeing King Kong's apparent gentleness fondling the Fay Wray of literature in his hairy grasp. He feigns sensibility throughout in his brutish, overweening style. Underneath the cultural winsomeness, there is the bully, the brute. And a bully he is, hurling tiresome mnemonics, dull word games and anagrams all about him, threatening maim if he is not understood. To the writing game, he is the head waiter who can speak seven languages with self-gratifying, uninteresting pedantry and no talent for the merest service.

Reading any of his works, and *Pale Fire* in particular,

he is one of the few writers who emerge as being down-right, irredeemably disagreeable and someone to avoid in the club or at dinner. He behaves as if he has discarded the heritage of Russian literature, but brought its content and memory in his own unique carpet-bag into exile.

As is too well-known, his hobby was lepidoptery, which implies an intellectual impishness and delicacy unknown to those who follow bull-fighting, flat-racing or darts. I don't like to think what he got up to with those butterflies. Someone, quite absurdly, called him a great poet of love. If this be love, it is something best not implied, let alone thought of, like paedophilia. He wrote his novels meticulously on card indexes, while his wife Vera looked over the inadequacies of the Turkish and Albanian translations of his masterworks in their Swiss hotel. The image of such a life is presumably meant to seem austere and impressive, though it is not dissimilar to that of a retired group captain and his wife in Eastbourne.

Pale Fire was alleged by Nabokov himself to be the hardest of his books to write, but it can't have compared with the pain of having to read it. A plodding and ponderous satire on academic pedantry, it is in three parts: a foreword by emigré Dr Kinbote to a posthumous poem by his "friend", the American poet and scholar John Shade; the four cantos of the poem itself and, finally, Kinbote's overblown commentary. Kinbote turns out to be the poufy deposed king, Charles Xavier the Beloved, of Zembla, some kind of gay Ruritania. Or does he? The blurb calls it "a sort of do-it-yourself detective story". Please yourself.

Shade is a saintly, put-upon literary hero, like his creator (after all, they *both* write meticulously on index cards). *Pale Fire* can therefore be taken — or not — as Nabokov's revenge at being picked over by minds less flashy and even more dully pedantic than his own, in this case the all too realistically boring Zembla-fixated Kinbote. The whole tome is shot through with a lowering jokiness, stuffed with knowing little references to the Nabokov canon. He modestly invokes Swift. As for the style, try these gob-stoppers for size: architectonic, nomenclatorial agitation, linden bosquet . . .

Or, from the master poem itself:

> Torquated beauty, sublimated grouse.
> Stilettos of a frozen stillicide.
> Too weary to delete, I drop my pen;
> I ambulate – and by some mute command
> The right word flutes and perches on my head.
> . . . And that odd muse of mine,
> My versipel, is with me everywhere,
> In carrel and in car, and in my chair.

(You're never alone with a versipel.)

Or, from the Commentary:

> Always at the same time the brown morocco slipper would drop from the wool-socked foot which continued to oscillate, with, however, a slight slackening of pace. One knew that bedtime was closing in with all its terrors; that in a few minutes the toe would prod and worry the slipper, and then disappear with it from my golden field of vision traversed by the black bendlet of a branch. . . .
>
> It confused a green monocle with an opaque occulent. . . .
>
> When stripped and shiny in the midst of the bath house, his bold virilia contrasted harshly with his girlish grace. He was a regular faunlet. . . .

Or, for that matter, whole pages which are virtually unreadable. Take, for instance, at random from the Penguin edition, pages 125, 126 or 127.

Can there be any voice raised in mitigation, even from Academe, when confronted with the evidence of such grievous bodily harm to the English tongue? Take that Russian exile's card-index system away! What will he do when he gets his hand on a silicon chip? Unscramble the English language altogether?

Some years ago, Nabokov was asked: "Are you a 'nostalgist'? In what time would you prefer to live?"

He replied: "In the coming days of silent planes and graceful aircycles, and cloudless silvery skies, and a universal system of padded underground roads to which trucks shall be relegated like Morlocks. As to the past, I would not mind retrieving from various corners of space-time certain lost comforts, such as baggy trousers and long, deep bath-tubs."

My first wife sometimes wrote like that after too much Dubonnet and Dylan Thomas.

He was also asked: "Do you consider yourself American?"

He replied: "Yes I do. I am as American as April in Arizona."

Now, even as a German-American student, spinning somewhere out in English literature, would you really buy a used book from such a displaced bullshit artist?

Vladimir Nabokov, Pale Fire *(first published 1962), Penguin, 1981*

STEVE RACE
Snobbery with Violence

"See what Auntie Lena has brought you for Christmas," said my mother.

"It's a book," I said. (I was six. I liked books.)

"Oh how lovely! Which book?"

I tore off the last covering of brown paper. "Oh," I said. "It's only a Bible."

I can remember the silence. Auntie Lena, I could see, was displeased. But she must have taken my disappointment to heart, because next year the book I unwrapped was *Alice's Adventures in Wonderland*. I can't say I enjoyed it any more, finding both of them heavy on violence and given to moralising. Though at least the Bible carried an undercurrent of love that was oddly lacking from Lewis Carroll's book.

Don't get me wrong. I love whimsy. Let no one try to steal my copy of *The Wind in the Willows* or my tear-stained *The House at Pooh Corner*. I don't object to strong action, tragedy, even stark horror. Goodness me, if one can face the thought of Eeyore floating upside-down and inert under the poohsticks bridge, or of Piglet bursting his one-and-only balloon, one has faced life at its most brutal.

But *Alice* I did *not* enjoy, at the age of six, sixteen, or even now at sixty. "She had read several nice little stories about children who had got burnt," comments Lewis Carroll with relish on page sixteen of my edition, "eaten up by wild beasts and other unpleasant things." And soon we are learning about Alice's "dear little cat Dinah", who will "eat a little bird as soon as look at it". An upset goldfish bowl results in the fish "sprawling about". And even the dormouse, in order to be awakened from sleep, has to be "pinched on both sides at once".

As for live hedgehogs serving as croquet balls to be struck by live flamingoes as mallets, the concept strikes me as unbeamish to a degree. The grim slapstick reaches its climax when the cook snatches hot soup from the fire to hurl it at the Duchess and her miserable baby . . . Not that the baby (howling by now) is a baby at all, but a hideously transmuted pig. Funsville.

I shall be told that children adore cruelty and violence, and I can only reply that this child didn't when the violence was as insidious and as pitiless as in *Alice*. And the snobbery! Alice's little friend Mabel, who "lives in a poky house" back in the real world, may briefly engage our sympathies. But when Alice is asked why her shoes are so shiny she replies, "They're done with blacking, *I believe*," showing a very proper ignorance of what goes on below stairs. It reminds one of Wilde's Hon. Gwendolen Fairfax, invited to call a spade a spade, replying that she was glad to say she had never seen a spade.

Alice, the classic little know-all, is fond of nitpicking word-play, as indeed are almost all the characters she meets. So different at first in description and appearance, they always end up arguing petulantly about what was meant as opposed to what was said.

Then finally we reach the gooey postscript, in which our heroine's big sister dreams how ". . . the same little sister of hers would, in the after-time . . . keep through all her riper years the simple and loving heart of her childhood . . ." Yuk! Off with her head, say I.

I'm not sure I ever got as far as that at first reading. Or even at second reading . . . Because by then I'd turned back to the previous year's gift, and found some quite interesting bits in the Bible that Auntie Lena can't possibly have known were there.

Lewis Carroll, Alice's Adventures in Wonderland *(first published 1865), Purnell, 1979*
Kenneth Grahame, The Wind in the Willows *(first published 1908), Methuen*
A. A. Milne, The House at Pooh Corner *(first published 1928), Methuen, 1965*

FREDERIC RAPHAEL
Authorised Version

"Faut-il brûler ...?" is a question older even than French. It begins with Plato, which is why, in the tradition which decrees that those who devise engines of subtle execution should be the first to perish in them, I am disposed to make *The Republic* my recommendation for the censorious flames. The fact that it has a certain beauty makes it only the more regrettable that, as the rugger buggers say, it was ever born at all.

Not the least damning, if retrospective, reproach against Plato's seminal book is, precisely, the seed that it has sown. His apologists retort that *The Republic* was never intended to be a practical guide-book for the magistrate, the *gauleiter* or the Independent Television Authority; it was meant only to be an impartial examination of the logic of a perfect polity, were perfection possible, or impartiality. An unpremeditated reading gives no such impression of dispassionate speculation. The tone is vigorously, and entertainingly, polemical; targets above the belt do not greatly interest its author. The satire on political systems is splendidly comic and apparently immune to rust; the typology of politicians is witty, cruel and instantly recognisable.

Nevertheless, the image of Plato as a philosopher so long in the neck that his noble head cannot but be in the clouds has been ardently preserved by those who insist on seeing their favourite metaphysician as an other-worldly precursor of Christianity. The joyless City of God is mirrored in the unsmiling city of man (Plato warns strongly against loud laughter, the worst medicine). The "noble lie" involved in founding a state based on the class system has been defended, with varying degrees of brazenness and good faith, by those who maintain that it was really meant to be a sort of patriotic fiction, but the fact remains that no philosopher before

Plato made it an essential element of the cult of truth that it should be founded on a falsehood. He has been so laurelled with hardy accolades that his penchant for dirty pool has been as rarely remarked as his casual invocation of the death penalty for misfits.

He affected to be scandalised by the ribald view which Homer and Aeschylus took of the gods and he proposed, on that supposedly reluctant account, to ban their works from the ideal city. Was his piety really so considerate of divine feelings or eternal verities? I suspect that envy played as great a part in his verdict as morals. His ideas have made humbug a civic virtue and creative impotence a ground for self-esteem.

Generations of clerks have praised his dramatic skill (the entrance of Thrasymachus is certainly well timed), but they rather overdo it when they claim that he too could have been a master dramatist, had he not been so busy with the Good and the Beautiful. Whatever the early liveliness of his dialogues, he soon lost all interest in the vivid presentation of contrary voices. Indeed, his last work, *The Laws*, has passed an interdict against itself, so to speak, owing to the cranky self-righteousness by which it is marked.

I am far from thinking that the crucial test of art is its success with a mass audience, but the resentment shown by Plato towards those whose greatness was, so to speak, voted them by the applause of society leads him, virtually and virtuously, to close both the theatres and the bookshops. The "excesses" of democracy and of art so gloatingly delineated by the author of *The Republic* have been made the excuse for tyranny and censorship ever since. (It took two thousand years for a dishonourable Greek to honour Plato's wishes and ban Aristophanes.) The notion of a logical model for society has not only been perverted but is itself a perversion. That the most artful example of tendentious perversity is also one of the great essays and unavoidable texts of Western Thought, a blueprint which has dignified repression and authorised vanity, is certainly a pity and probably a tragedy, for it has continued to license political speculators to search for the unattainable, a search which in brutal practice (like so many crusades sponsored by metaphysics) has been as bloody as it has been fruitless.

Plato, The Republic *(first published 4th century B.C.),*
Penguin, 1970
The Laws *(first published 4th century B.C.), Penguin, 1970*

BRIAN REDHEAD

To Have or Have Not

Arnold Bennett bought a book every day. They were cheaper then, and he was richer. I buy a book every week, sometimes two, occasionally three. Real books not paperbacks. New books not second-hand. And I buy them not just to read but to have.

A book is more than the words it contains. Gutenberg, who did it first, said that a book embraces both the adventure of the author and the art of the printer. And the reader should admire the art before sharing the adventure.

I like to get to know a book before I read it. Just as I like a new suit to hang in the wardrobe for several weeks or months before I wear it.

I read two or three books at a time. They pile up on bedside tables and in the sitting room. Until newcomers gradually force them into shelves.

Books are to be kept not discarded. It's all right to cast off paperbacks, to read them on trains and leave them among the scattered newspapers in the hope that they will brighten the day of a carriage cleaner.

But real books are for keeping. A home without a book is only a house. It is a running joke in my home that a subject has only to be raised in conversation over dinner for me to disappear saying that I have a book on that.

And often I am not seen again, because I can't find the book in question but I've found another I had forgotten I had and am deep into it.

I buy books on the same principle. My choice is determined not by reviews, which I seldom read, but by chance. I often enter a shop with a book in mind, light upon another, and emerge with that.

So my anti-booklist is headed by those who would devalue the search, the art, and the adventure.

They litter the Sunday supplements – themselves no longer magazines, but mail-order catalogues – and offer instant libraries, bound in plastic.

They are anti-book.

And book clubs are not much better. They limit the choice to their subscribers and lure the innocent with cut-price offers of books which already lie unread on too many shelves.

It is all a conspiracy to sell more and more copies of fewer and fewer books.

One day there will be no libraries. Only a global book-shelf.

STANLEY REYNOLDS
Los Crapos

Well, you know how it used to be when Papa wrote the books early in the morning in Havana across the street from the sawmill with Scott and Zelda and Gertrude Stein and Mister Bumby and Hadley and Brett. They were all having a fine time down at the Dôme on the Boul, Bullsheet watching the fairies go by, which was not so very fine, which was actually and finally *nada* and *kaput* and totally lacking in *cojones* and failed to have the real and truly true *afición* without which it was nothing as Papa, who was a fine old man who had gone eighty-seven days without a novel and then finally wrote one but it was too big for his typewriter. And so he tied the novel to his typewriter. But the bulls came and gored it until they got tired of goring the novel and went to the Dôme and had a few drinks and that was good, the bulls said, and a lot better than goring the old man's novel which was basically and truly and finally rather boring. Well, Papa wrote standing up, and this was good and truly fine especially if you had a few drinks, but he had a hard time seeing the typewriter's keyboard because of all the hair on his chest. So that finally in the end he grew a big beard and it was fine that he no longer had to gaze down on the hair on his chest but still he could not see the typewriter keyboard, he could now only see his beard. And that was bad and rather *nada* and lacking in *cojones*. But after a few drinks it felt better, and the business of not seeing the letters on the typewriter was not so bad, except at night. Anyway, it is truly a great obscenity to try to pick the worst book which Papa wrote because all of them make you truly wish to foul in the milk of thy mother, *hombre*. If you are young and have never gone eighty-seven days without killing a bull and do not possess the passion or the *afición*, as Zelda used to say, which is just the Spanish word for passion but that was the way Zelda was, and when Scott learned Spanish too she forgot all her Spanish and never said *afición* ever again but spoke only in Serbo-Croatian especially when she was drunk which was all the time when she wasn't stinko. That was the trouble with Scott, that and the fact that the barman at the Ritz could never remember his name. If you are young and do not know all this you will think *The Sun Also Rises* is a bad book which is to say it is not good or even truly fine. But this was only Papa's first novel and he was only twenty-six, which is to say he was young, and he did not know much then. It was only later that he learned to write the truly ungood books which are of such an awfulness that it goes beyond mentioning the obscenity of them and the number of young writers who were wounded trying to imitate them and whose sentences would go on limping for the rest of their lives. Afterwards it was enough to just say the names of the novels. *For Whom The Bell Tolls* was truly a very unfine book and today it is difficult to read it without laughing well and truly and finally out loud except that you remember how many young men read it and lost all their adjectives and that wipes the smile off your face until you have a few drinks and then it is fine and Brett and Pilar and Maria and that appalling wooden nurse from *A Farewell to Arms* come into the Dôme not wearing bras. And the old man, who was a fine old man, said *"See nipples and die"* and we all laughed and it was good and then we all caught some fine fish and thought about the war and it was good. But that was only the First World War or maybe the Spanish Civil War and it was all very fine thinking about that. But Papa's finest hour came with the Second World War when he wrote a novel of such unspeakable awfulness that even the young writers who had cut off their own adjectives to be what the Spanish call *sin adjectivos* (which is the sparsest of sparse as far as style goes), started believing that maybe the old man was just full of bullshit after all. Of course now we all know that Papa was full of what the Spanish call *los crapos* but then it was different. When *Across the River and into the Trees* came out with the boring old colonel falling in love with the appalling Italian countess, who was well and truly even more wooden than any of Papa's other female characters, people started getting wise. I remember it well. We were all sitting in the Café Jean Genet, Zelda, Scott, Gertrude Stein, Brett, and Henry Miller said, "Papa has got no adjectives but is that enough?"

"No, truly," Jack Kerouac said, "that is not enough."

Then we all went across the street and into the bar and had a few drinks and got tight and used a lot of adjectives and it was good and truly fine to be rid of the old bore at long last.

Ernest Hemingway, The Sun Also Rises *(US title),* Fiesta *(UK title), (first published 1926), Panther, 1976*
For Whom The Bell Tolls *(first published 1940), Panther, 1976*
A Farewell to Arms *(first published 1929), Panther, 1977*
Across the River and into the Trees *(first published 1950), Panther, 1977*

HILARY RUBINSTEIN
Unclean! Unclean!

Leviticus, schleviticus. Who reads the Third Book of Moses anyway?

Far more than you might imagine. Thanks to Mr Gideon, the Bible is frequently the only literature available in a million or more hotel rooms throughout the world. I doubt whether any other work in *The Anti-Book List* has a comparable circulation; and none can be so frequently the recourse of jet-confused insomniacs desperate for something to read in the small hours.

At a cursory glance, Leviticus is concerned with primitive regulations on rituals and sacrifices, of little contemporary relevance. But it is no accident that the book has often been compulsory reading in the dormitories of single-sex boarding schools after lights out. Consider, for instance, those pernicious verses 16–18 of chapter 15:

> If any man's seed of copulation go out from him, then he shall wash all his flesh in water, and be unclean until the even. And every garment, and every skin, whereon is the seed of copulation, shall be washed with water and be unclean until the even. The woman also with whom man shall lie with seed of copulation, they shall both bathe themselves with water and be unclean until the even.

You can just hear the sniggers. And it isn't just copulation that is unclean, menstruation also becomes a defilement, so that anyone who touches the "woman with an issue" or her clothes or even her bed or her chair, becomes an unclean person too.

Campaigners for sexual equality will raise their eyebrows or hackles at chapter 12, where the author of Leviticus lays down the period of uncleanliness after childbirth: seven days for a man child, two weeks for a maid child. In another passage, a man's vows may be redeemed for twenty shekels, and a woman's for ten . . . Gay libbers, too, get short shrift: "Thou shalt not lie with mankind as with womankind; it is abomination." And there are plenty of other cruel prohibitions: no man may marry a woman that has been "put away from her husband", and the high priest may not even marry a widow. Those with physical blemishes are treated as outcasts – "a blind man or a lame, or he that hath a flat nose or anything superfluous. Or a man that is broken-footed or brokenhanded".

Leviticus is rigidly authoritarian. It is obsessed with sin and guilt. "Thou shalt not" is the constant refrain, and a terrible retribution is in store for those who transgress. Chapter 26 contains the longest sustained curse in the Old Testament – twenty-seven verses of brimstone and treacle and worse for those who fail to keep the commandments. It is perhaps the earliest known document in the history of repression, an ancestral precursor of Mrs Whitehouse. There is no joy anywhere in the book, and precious little of the quality of mercy. It is the apotheosis of negativity – surely the first and ultimate anti-book?

The Book of Leviticus, *the third book of the Old Testament, may date (in part) from the thirteenth century B.C.*

MICHAEL SCHMIDT
Shadowy Puppets

There are many books I dislike, few I would wish unwritten. Usually a bad book declares itself early, like an uncongenial guest. At the first opportunity you move away and engage someone else in conversation. I find books of literary theory avoidable: if you persist with some of them, you come out knowing less than when you went in. Bad books narrow the understanding, but one can side-step them.

There is a kind of badness that used to be called *evil*, and I do know one *evil* book. I wish I had not read it. I wish it could be unwritten. I threw it out ten years back, but my aversion to it remains strong, perhaps because it meant so much to me (as did other work by the same author) when I was an adolescent. The bad book is *L'Immoraliste* (1902) and the author André Gide.

Gide sets out to disturb his reader, but like the irresponsible satirist who discredits values or institutions without suggesting improvements or viable alternatives, so Gide disturbs for disturbance's sake, leaving especially the susceptible adolescent reader in a delicious-seeming moral wilderness. It is quite possible to get lost there.

The problem is that Gide was busy making personal, spiritual, sexual, social and political choices throughout his work. A better writer would have presented rather than made the choices. Gide is out for gratification and justification; he is an oblique and furtive pornographer, playing with his reader; a propagandist withholding his true motive, masking his seduction. He romanticises and makes sultry the kind of human *cul-de-sac* that Thomas Mann makes terrible and real in his novellas, or that Kafka schematises nightmarishly in his stories. Gide sentimentalises evil; his characters are in close-up and we have no perspective on their action, no sense of its human consequences. The failure of his fiction is his inability finally to attach his obsessive ideas to his shadowy puppets. The scene is real, the ideas evidently felt, but nothing is embodied; "characters" are clauses in an idea, parts of a proof. He may in the end be a pagan, but if so he is a dull one: a pagan without spiritual conflict, without any context left, unable to add one experience to another.

Yet how deliciously those palm trees waved, and how conveniently the wife died, too, and the Arab lads with their available sisters filled in an existence entirely foregrounded, entirely self-indulged!

André Gide, L'Immoraliste *(first published 1902), Penguin, 1970*

AUDREY SLAUGHTER

Second-Hand Sword

Books I *dislike* . . . would I ever finish them? There are so
many I want to read stretching through library and
bookshop shelves. Why should I waste time on dislike-
able books?

The one I ought to dislike, I suppose, is Anne Scott-
James's *In the Mink*. What a bad effect that had on me!
From the first page when she went for an interview at
Venus magazine (despite her disclaimer in the foreword
I knew it was *Vogue*) and was told, "You have absolutely
no experience, and you are not well dressed, but you can
spell and your shoes are good," I was hooked. I wasn't
well dressed, I had no experience, I could spell and I
thought my shoes were good – serviceable but good –
and journalism beckoned.

Up until *In the Mink* I'd planned to work for a Walter
Matthau character on a newspaper who gritted "Hold
the Front Page" as I phoned my story from a bullet-
strewn airfield in the desert. Liz Gaskell showed me
Gracious Living in all its awful fascination. Mrs van
Elder didn't put me off:

> She was nearly six feet tall and emaciatedly thin, with short
> dark hair and protruding teeth. She wore a tight black suit,
> black hat and high white blouse and clanked with gold
> jewellery as she moved. She struck me as repulsive. "That
> was Mrs van Elder, the merchandise editor," said Rosie.
> "The chicest woman here."

At school, red-haired and freckled, I'd read glossy
magazines voraciously faintly hoping that beauty and
allure would be mine if I followed their dictates. I once
went to the school dance looking a perfect freak having
obediently "Sellotaped a rose to my bare shoulder". The
attraction of a boney adolescent shoulder with a precari-

ously bobbing rose seemed to escape the boys lining the wall.

Though *In the Mink* was meant to be a piece of fiction to protect the innocent, I knew that if from inside the gauche Liz Gaskell the elegant sophisticated author Anne Scott-James struggled out, it could happen to me.

Liz Gaskell's first job was anglicising a piece from their American edition. It went:

TRY THESE FOR FALL

Take a friend's child to Sunday school.
Wear something red at your throat, your waist your feet
Reread Forsyte Saga
Have something taffeta for fall, spiced, surprisingly, with fur
Play Sibelius records for one whole evening and hand Turkish cigarettes

and so on. (If that has a familiar ring, they're still at it.)

In the Mink gently sent up the world of glossy magazines, but I didn't spot it then. I was too anxious to join in and wear red at my throat (blood?) and drift languidly round smart parties sipping pink champagne. So I wrote to the editor of *Vogue*, then Audrey Withers, and was sick with nerves when she asked me to go for an interview. Again Liz Gaskell described the scene exactly:

She looked at me as though I were a spider in the bath.
I became hotly conscious of my gangling appearance.
I felt all arms and legs. My scarlet jersey looked abominably coarse beside her pleated white lawn blouse, and my longish hair wispy with her neat dark curls . . .

I didn't get the job with *Vogue*, but I wasn't put off. *In the Mink* was peopled by bizarre, eccentric, neurotic characters, riven by internecine strife but, naturally, so talented, all was forgiven. I wanted to join them. Imagine the challenge of an art director scribbling an instruction: "Your title too short. Must be thirteen words; first word must be of one letter. We must have two twelve-letter words in the middle."

And Amy Sweet – how I wanted to have a friend like

Amy Sweet who wore an enormous Russian fur hat indoors because it was comfortable, and described her flat, crammed with bric-à-brac and Victorian furniture and plants and books, as "functional"; who lunched exquisitely on gulls' eggs and had a scimitar on her front door as a knocker. My friends seemed to have thick red calves and play tennis. The second-hand sword I finally banged in place as a door knocker was ignored in favour of the landlady's cheap electric bell.

Thanks to *In the Mink* I did join a magazine. It wasn't *Vogue*. It wasn't anything *like* it. The women still had red calves. There were no clever homosexual photographers with "hooded, secret eyes" to gossip deliciously with — as *In the Mink* — just an eighty-year-old home editor whose pages were designed for suburban semis. The editor wore Women's Institute clothes, had grey hair worn in a straggling bun, and had a deaf aid which she switched off when you disagreed with her. Instead of creative art directors demanding beautifully-tailored headings I wrote to order depressing titles like "Easy to knit dress in simple stocking stitch". It was a great comedown. So, you see, *In the Mink* almost ruined my life.

Anne Scott-James, In the Mink, *Michael Joseph, 1952*

ANNE SMITH

The Lady and the Tramp

It's when you're in bed with flu and beyond the reach of excuses that the Presbyterian creed of justification by works comes into its own. Chastened by a sense of impending Judgment, I surround myself with duty-books, the number of which is in inverse ratio to the severity of the complaint – I've rattled at death's door with *Studs Lonigan* unfinished in my hand half a dozen times now: it is to me what Foxe's *Book of Martyrs* must have been to a Victorian child on a wet Sunday.

The last dose was a milder, two-book flu. For two days I hovered between Lawrence's *The Trespasser* and Barbara Cartland's *The Hell-Cat and the King*, turning from the tortured perusal of "... in the darkness something magnetic passed between them which she could not explain" to "In an instant he was kneeling, and she was lying on his shoulder, abandoned to him." I leave the quotations unidentified with a certain sadistic pleasure, but am forced to admit that when it comes to awfulness Barbara Cartland wins hands down.

She writes, to paraphrase John Aubrey, as a boar pisseth – by jerks. Some teacher of English must be even now roasting in a grammarian's hell for failing to instruct Miss Cartland in the difference between a sentence and a paragraph. I suspect he got into her school under false pretences, having spent his formative years composing sentences for translation into Latin by schoolboys of ten and under: "From the sea Trieste looked impressive and she remembered that the port had been founded by Julius Caesar, although she was quite certain few people knew that today."

This, I fear, is the long-lost novel of Oscar Wilde's Miss Prism; it is the Great Tradition told by an idiot: " 'Why was I not born a boy?' Zenka asked herself. Then she realised if she had been, none of these problems would have arisen.

"Then she told herself she was merely being imaginative and such things did not happen in the nineteenth century."

I know two other people who have read Barbara Cartland. One is a friend who went to convent school. She tells me that she and her peers read BC under the desk-lid for its pornographic value, much as my peers and I read *Lady Chatterley's Lover*. In terms of titillation the convent had the better of the deal, for these novels are masturbatory fantasies stopping short of physical detail. Helena, the heroine of *The Trespasser*, would have been the ideal BC reader perhaps: "She belonged to that class of 'dreaming women' with whom passion exhausts itself at the mouth. Her desire was accomplished in a simple kiss." Prick-teasing in ten easy lessons. (But there *is* a rape in one of the 'novels').

The other friend was a judge, who braved BC in his maturer years. There is no record of which of the many millions of her books he chose to read, since after half an hour's ominous rumblings he clashed it into the heart of the fire, loudly denouncing Miss Cartland for obscenity. Inured in my youth to erotic fantasy that stops short of the useful detail through frequent close readings of Hank Janson and Paul Renin – and the phallic mythology is the same after all: it's the penis as magic wand; one touch of Ian's rough Scottish magic and you're his for life – her sexual brinkmanship leaves me unmoved. What made me feed *The Hell-Cat and the King* into the central-heating boiler was the outrage of reading five successive sentence/paragraphs starting with "She had . . ."

The Trespasser bids well to follow: I've just struggled through a description of Helena's – mind? – which goes:

> "That yellow flower hadn't time to be brushed and combed by the fairies before dawn came. It is tousled . . ." so she thought to herself. The pink convolvuli were fairy horns or telephones from the day fairies to the night fairies. The rippling sunlight on the sea was the Rhine maidens spreading their bright hair to the sun. That was her favourite form of thinking.

Quite clearly this is the literary source of Wodehouse's Madeleine Bassett, who thought that every time a fairy sneezed a wee baby was born . . .

J. T. Farrell, Studs Lonigan *(first published 1932-5), Panther, 1979*
Foxe's Book of Martyrs *(1563)*
D. H. Lawrence, The Trespasser *(first published 1912), Penguin, 1970*
Barbara Cartland, The Hell-Cat and the King, *Pan, 1978*

ANTHONY SMITH
Textual Criticism

The idea of listing hated books does not have immediate appeal. Why hate a piece of creation even if it is at the bottom end of one's own appreciation scale? Why not just put that particular book aside and let its contents remain secure within their covers, disliked certainly – but hated? Even *Mein Kampf* can be admired for its straightforwardness, *Uncle Tom's Cabin* for its place in history and, as for Dorothy Parker's so stern indictment of Winnie the Pooh and her alleged throwing-up, that too did not imply hatred.

I think the nearest I have come to loathing is with textbooks, and for two reasons: they were compulsory reading, and they frequently succeeded – to use Aldous Huxley's "inverted alchemy" – in turning all the gold of this world into lead. I did not, and do not, see why they had to be so dull, and I certainly resented them for it. They, above all else, represented the educational system of sham pearls being cast before real swine. They took wondrous facts and transformed these into turgid lists, interspersed with pea-soup prose and dismal diagram. It was as if no excitement or joy should be set before a student, in case it might stimulate him or her into original thought, or happiness. Learning from a dreary text was proof both of application and of spirit. To spare this form of rod was to spoil the child.

They say that textbooks for today's pupils are better, just as they say that the schools are better. I hope they are, and that some of the more awful texts have been swept aside. I do not know which was the worst, as of course I encountered them at different ages and when differently equipped to object to them; but I think the largest seal of disapproval should be awarded to those enforced upon the older, more discriminating but still fettered student, such as those in their middle teens. I was then subjected to C. J. Smith's *Intermediate Physics* and Holmyard's *Higher School Inorganic Chemistry*, but I think abyssal pride of place should go to L. A. Borradaile's *The Invertebrata*. It was also known as "Beps" because the thing was perpetrated not just by Borradaile but by L. E. S. Eastham, F. A. Potts and J. T. Saunders (and was published by the Cambridge University Press, originally in 1932).

Why did I dislike it so much? Well, it changed the wonder of the invertebrate world into indigestible Latinised tedium. How's this for openers as its very first sentence? "The Invertebrata have long since ceased to constitute one of the primary divisions in the scientific classification of the Animal Kingdom." What was the book's title again, and how's that for an immediate rebuff? However it never lets up: "This type is said to possess the *caridoid facies*." "The Protozoa are sundered from the rest of the Animal Kingdom . . ." "Of the appendages or limbs of the Crustacea, the first, or

atennule, is a structure *sui generis* . . ." Coupled with such porridge were occasional, but always nasty, little drawings that also sought to uninspire. It was a book to be resented, deeply, for its lack of warmth, of life, of feeling, but the fact that it was compulsory reading did, I suppose, depress one's considerable dislike into a form of hatred. I have certainly not enjoyed collecting it from the library to refresh my memory of its particular depths, a nadir that so many others have tried to emulate but few, happily, have achieved quite so well.

Adolf Hitler, Mein Kampf *(first published 1925-6), Hutchinson, 1972*

Harriet Beecher Stowe, Uncle Tom's Cabin *(first published 1851-2), Dent, 1972*

E. J. Holmyard and W. G. Palmer, Higher School Inorganic Chemistry, *Dent, 1964*

L. A. Borradaile, L. E. S. Eastham, F. A. Potts, J. T. Saunders, The Invertebrata (first published 1932), CUP, 1961

GODFREY SMITH
Madness, Do You Hear?

"We are in the tower of Sissinghurst Castle. In the turret room where his mother, the writer Vita Sackville-West, always worked, her son and executor finds a locked Gladstone bag. There is no key, so he cuts through the leather with a knife: 'the bag contained something – a tiara in its case, for all I knew.' Within, he finds a large notebook, filled with his dead mother's neat, pencilled writing. 'I read it through to the end without stirring . . . It was an autobiography written when she was aged twenty-eight, a confession, an attempt to purge her mind and heart of a love which had possessed her, a love for another woman, Violet Trefusis."

It is a sizzling start, and Nigel Nicolson is much too good an editor – and writer – to muff his chance. The book which was to emerge from this Gothic find is admirably arranged. Vita's manuscript is split into two sections, each followed by a commentary by Nigel which amplifies and decodes. A fifth and final section by Nigel rounds out the story. He does it with candour and elegance.

What on earth, then, is the case against the book? Is it a betrayal of his mother's confessional? Surely not: all the internal evidence points to her wish for eventual publication. Is it then, too pat a celebration of Lesbianism? In today's context, that is a laughable charge. Is it no more than an apologia for marital infidelity? Yes, but the case is not put lightly; nor badly. Well then?

The key to the case against the book is buried halfway down page 114. At the very pitch of the tempestuous affair, Vita calls early one morning to say goodbye to Violet. In her own words: "There was a dreary slut scrubbing the doorstep, for it was very early, and I stepped in over the soapy pail, and saw Violet in the morning room. Then I went to Paris alone."

The luxuriant ecstasy so eloquently chronicled by both women is a function of ludicrous privilege and an exercise in self-indulgence which is emetic in its ruthlessness. "Where is the money to come from?" wrote Vita's mother, Lady Sackville, when the young diplomat Harold Nicolson wanted to marry her (unaware that she was already having it away with her future bridesmaid Rosamund Grosvenor). The answer was that it would be supplied by the will of twenty-five-stone Sir John Murray Scott, the mother's unwavering admirer (though at that weight not much else) and would finance the hysterical flights abroad, the shower of telegrams in French to fox the local postmistress, the shattering scenes in foreign hotels, the callous indifference to the two husbands ("he cares for me drivellingly" Violet wrote contemptuously of her tear-stained and pathetic Denys).

Harold Nicolson is the true hero of the sordid chronicle: balanced, patient, civilised. Yet even his reserve sometimes cracked: "Darling, she is evil" he wrote to Vita of Violet "and I am not evil." He sent them a hard-earned £130 when they ran out of cash gambling in Monte Carlo. "I will show you madness, Vita, (madness, do you hear?)" Violet hammed, "Let's live, you and I, as none have ever lived before." Boloney: they were two hopelessly spoiled upper-class bitches on a monumental and reciprocal ego trip. Meanwhile Harold was away working on the Versailles Peace Treaty. He was appointed to the new League of Nations; but Vita had never heard of the League. She was too busy living: if that is what it was.

Nigel Nicolson, Portrait of a Marriage: Vita Sackville-West and Harold Nicolson *(first published 1973), Futura, 1975*

JOHN TIMPSON

Why It Never Got Out

Every journalist has a great novel within him. Every journalist has an excellent reason why it never got out. My own downfall was *Roget's Thesaurus*. We have had a love-hate relationship ever since.

The difficulties with the *Thesaurus* start when you try to pronounce it. I could not decide for years between the brontosaurus approach (what a title for a horror movie, *Thesaurus Wakes*), or stressing the first syllable to rhyme it with pessaries. The second version could be varied by ignoring the "h", as in "thyme", thus creating a vision of *Thesaurus* of the d'Urbervilles. As to which is correct, your Thesaurus is as good as mine.

But the real problems start inside the covers. To get to the *Thesaurus* itself you have to negotiate the Plan of Classification, the Tabular Synopsis of Categories, one foreword, three prefaces and an introduction, mostly written by descendants of the original Dr Roget and all saying what a jolly good book this is. There is also, mercifully, a section called "How To Use This Book", which incidentally is the only sentence in the entire volume limited to words of one syllable.

Think of a word, it explains, then consult the *Thesaurus* and a multitude of alternative words will forthwith spring to the eye. They are arranged "so as to facilitate the expression of ideas and to assist in literary composition", and it was this which ensnared me. When I embarked on the great novel, any hesitation over a *mot juste* and in a trice Dr Roget would fill the gap, leaving my mind free to conjure up more fine fantasies and express more great thoughts. The *Thesaurus* would take the mechanics out of composition; it was the early equivalent of a literary micro-chip.

But the good doctor is not quite as straightforward as that. To step into his pages in search of a word is like plunging into a marsh in pursuit of a will-o'-the-wisp. Long before you catch it you will be bogged down along false trails, your original purpose forgotten, your train of thought gone.

Suppose, for instance, I seek another word for *Thesaurus*, which has already been much overworked. The index offers one main route and four side paths, labelled "List", "Book", "Words" and "Store". Each one may have something to offer, but the main route comes first.

"Treasury", it says. It is a possible; but hang on. "Bank," it says, "exchequer, almonry, safe, strongbox, coffer, hanaper, porte-monnaie." This surely is not the path I seek. And "hanaper"? All right for *Call My Bluff*, but hardly helpful here. So how about the "list" group.

"Directory, gazetteer, dictionary, glossary, compendium . . ." Very nearly; but then it veers off again. "Scroll, manifest, bill of lading, menu . . ."

Try "book" – this must be it. "Volume, tome, opuscule, tract, treatise, codex, manual." It might be impressive to use "opuscule", but it would be as well to check first in the dictionary (let alone the gazetteer, directory, glossary, compendium). An opuscule, it seems, is a small or insignificant artistic work. Exasperating though the *Thesaurus* is, it is neither small nor insignificant. We are in shifting sands again.

"Words" ought to offer some hope, but in this group we are back to dictionaries again, and the Roget family in their assorted prefaces make it clear that their *Thesaurus* is not a dictionary. The final path, "store", is the most rambling of all, disappearing into a maze of warehouses, granaries, arsenals, conservatories, gasometers and zoological gardens. There is no joy there.

So we limp back to where we started, the mind filled with Dr Roget's well-meaning suggestions, none of which is precisely what we want. Yet it is a process which holds a terrible fascination for anyone whose business is with words. And thus it was that my great novel disappeared without trace under the spell of the *Thesaurus*, as I wandered off again and again through this etymological orchard, grasping for words which were constantly just out of reach. Well, not quite etymological. Perhaps lexicological, phonological, logoleptic, glossographic – or see under word, intelligence; word, command; word, promise . . .

Paul Mark Roget, Thesaurus of English Words and Phrases *(first published 1852), Penguin, 1966, Pan, 1972*

PETER TINNISWOOD

We Can't Have One

We can't have an aviary.

We have cats.

So do our neighbours.

Cats sit on the top of aviaries and frighten the birds. They prowl round the outside of the aviaries and scowl. Sometimes they just sit and stare.

I long for an aviary of foreign birds.

Right now I'd give anything to have one.

That's why I curse the publication of Mr Richard Mark Martin's *Cage and Aviary Birds*.

I wish him no harm. I wish him immense success, in fact. I wish him luck with his motmots and eternal happiness with his flower peckers.

But, dear Lord, his book has brought back memories and longings which have been dormant this past two decades.

When I was small with big ears I used to have an aviary.

My dad built it out of scrap timber and chicken wire.

The first two birds I bought were long-tailed grass finches.

They were sent by rail from Kent, and I collected them at Sale Station.

When I let them out of the box, they sat on a twig and moped.

They looked like the Italian prisoners of war we used to mock in their camps on Carrington Moss.

Then I bought a bronze-winged mannikin.

It escaped, and it sat in a plum tree all summer, looking smug.

Over the months I bought zebra finches, cuban finches, gouldian finches, and, best of all, a golden-fronted fruitsucker.

How it could sing.

The local blackbirds used to sit on the berberis hedge and gape in admiration.

I could have made a fortune hiring it out for singing lessons.

I used to sit in the garden in the summer and watch the weaver birds build nests out of the blue and red raffia we threw into the bottom of the aviary.

And the front-sucker would sing.

And the zebra finches would trumpet.

And I was quiet and contented.

That's what I'd like now.

I'd like my dad to build me an aviary out of scrap timber and chicken wire, and I'd stock it with combassous, paradise whydahs, java sparrows, diamond doves, red avadavats, orange-cheeked waxbills, red-naped widow birds and Chinese painted quail.

But I can't.

We have cats.

And so do our neighbours.

So I'll build an aviary and I'll stick Mr Martin's book in it.

I wonder if it would try to escape?

Richard Mark Martin, Cage and Aviary Birds, *Collins, 1980*

POLLY TOYNBEE

Dear Superwoman

I was really thrilled when my mother-in-law gave me
your book as a wedding present, hand-tooled in wash-
able leatherette. It felt a bit like being presented with the
Girl Guide Handbook when I was enrolled.

I must admit things haven't gone too well since then.
In your immortal opening lines you write, "The purpose
of this book is to help you do the work you don't like as
fast as possible, leaving time for the work you enjoy."
Five years later I'm still at it, doing the work I don't like
as fast as ever I can, but I never seem to get to the other
bit. Is there something the matter with me?

I have kept to your weekly rota faithfully: on Mondays
I defrost the fridge, clean the oven, scrub the dustbins
and the kitchen floor and do the household paperwork.
On Tuesdays I do the washing, ironing, mending,
shopping and dry cleaning, and so on through the week.
I do keep the eleven different household cleaners you list
always handy. I've used your tips from the Ritz
cloakroom lady on how to polish silver hairbrushes. I
wash my light bulbs, every one, every week, because you
say that you can lose twenty-five per cent of your light
with a grimy bulb, and I soak my acrylic lampshades in
the bath. Thank you for the tips on polishing the brass
inlay on antique furniture. I've had a bit of trouble finding
a stone marmalade jar to keep my lavatory brush in,
though. I'm sure you're right that you can't really see
kitchen-floor dirt unless you scrub it on your hands and
knees, so of course I do.

You're absolutely right that denture cleaner works
wonders on the silver teapot. I'm afraid I didn't follow
your dyeing instructions as well as I ought, and my
attempts at turning the sheets, towels and my own
underwear to the sexy coffee colour you suggest weren't
all I'd hoped for. I saved to buy the freezer you

recommended, which you said paid for itself in food economies in two years. I've grown rather fond of the half cow in the bottom, she's almost a pet. I never did quite get round to filling it with the *blanquette de veau* and *coq au vin* that you always keep handy for when your husband's boss drops in unexpectedly.

The other day we moved house and I followed your instructions to the letter. I made a complete plan of both houses, with every piece of furniture marked on each, and I labelled every object in the house for the movers. I remembered the emergency suitcase with a rubber plug and a torch. I informed the police we'd be parking on a yellow line. All the same, I did need The Working Girl's Toolbox, with its twenty-eight indispensables, as well as the ten different types of glue no home should be without. I didn't forget the binoculars for inspecting the roof and chimney stack.

You call your book "A Guide to Household Management for Today's Woman". And what a daunting task the modern woman has! Superwoman indeed! She goes to work, keeps the house spotless, entertains perfectly, has happy, loved and loving children, an immaculate filing system, notebooks and organisation. In your chapter on maintenance you say, "You were probably brought up to think they (maintenance jobs) are not a woman's work, but there isn't always a man about and it's probably easier to do it yourself than nag him into doing it." So now I too can unblock drains, mend fuses, stop taps leaking, put up shelves, change a tyre etc.

You write: "If you're lucky enough to have access to a man who can not only fix things around the home but is willing to do so, treat him gently and feed him well . . . Men are extremely good at being helpless. The cleverer they are the more helpless they are, and the cleverest ones prove this neatly by making things worse. Anyway you don't want to find yourself patching up a marriage." My husband's awfully clever – at least I suppose he must be.

But as I hinted at the beginning, things have not gone well. I feel I am unworthy, so I am returning the book, together with the Superwoman Badge of Merit sash.

Incidentally, I looked up Divorce in the index – but it goes straight from Dining Room Carpets, Dipstick, Dishcloths (boiling), and Dishwashers, to Documents, Dogs, Doorknobs and Double Glazing. I was surprised!
Yours sincerely,
A READER.

Shirley Conran, Superwoman: Every Woman's Book of Household Management *(first published 1975), Penguin, 1977*

JOHN VAIZEY
Twee Trolley

The pitiful state of British cooking, public and private, in the days of austerity, made it useful to have a hand list of places where the food that was sold was at least edible, and this was the origin of *The Good Food Guide*. Restaurant standards began to go up when the Cypriots arrived just after the war and put vine leaves round the mince. Then the Asians arrived. At least the food was spicy and cheap even if, as was commonly supposed, the ingredients were hotly disguised stewed rat, fried cat or boiled mat. The Chinese invented a new form of torture – raw bits of vegetable which, once ingested, swelled up and gave a feeling of repletion, leading shortly afterwards to famine on an oriental scale. In this United Nations of cookery some handy guide was useful, especially when passing the night in (say) Manchester. But I cannot think of a more vile, positively cloacal book than *The Good Food Guide*, essential though it sometimes is.

There is something inherently disgusting and even gross about the idea of going out to gorge. Home perm frozen to her head, diamanté glasses glistening, ill-chosen lipstick smudged, the expense account wife slobbers over her "carcass of local lamb that has been hung for four, eleven or eighteen days" (Windermere), not to mention the "hortobaggi pancake with spinach" (Greek Street), and, her long, dank, unwashed head bent over the pottery plate, ethnic beads clanking with the chopsticks, the *Guardian*-reading female (or indeed possibly male) social worker raises Trotskyitically her "samosa, bhajia and mung dhal balls" (London N.W.10) to her lips chapped from shouting a thousand shouts against police oppression on that day's demo.

Eating as I do at clubs, the House of Lords, or at the University, where the food usually tastes as though it had been cooked by a spinster headmistress temporarily without help in the house, the emphasis is naturally, and as it should be, on conversation, gossip and drink. Nobody who lunches or dines there can ever remember what they have eaten, rarely indeed what they have ordered, as the staff hand out food at random to apparently satisfied clients. The idea of turning up at the House of Lords because "terrine of turbot and sole with *beurre blanc* sauce and suissesses" (Ullswater) was on the menu is preposterous.

The hand list of where it was possible to eat if away from the House of Lords has become a paean of praise for a mixture of greed and sanctimonious uplift. Fish and chips, one feels, should always be wrapped in *Time Out* to be both edible and morally acceptable. "Vaunda Corindalet (who cooks) and her sister Eleanor Wragg succeeded a short-lived régime in this Georgian cottage by the church late in 1978, and have attracted notice for the obvious affection with which they are serving a judiciously modest range of food and wine." (Ottery St Mary). Analyse this passage carefully. They are not in it for the money. It is a non-profit-making way of life, almost a social service. The cottage is antique. "Girls serve in a natural manner, and Mr Kingsley 'in a piratical beard' expounds his English wines" (Richmond) runs another entry about a "parsonage style kitchen in the shadow of the parish church".

The essential tweeness of the entries, together with an obsessive interest in food, contrasts with the more brutal style of the French, who offer knives and forks and the occasional rosette, so that you know where you can eat well but have no need to *feel* it, to *experience* it, to *savour* it too. "There is no choice at dinner (with punctuality 'requested and observed as from one good cook to another') and where the service can only be compared with 'old-fashioned butlering'" (Oughterard). Bloody nerve. I almost prefer the Alsatian restaurant in a tastefully converted warehouse fronting on Castlebar's car park.

The absurdity and vulgarity of the pursuit of transitory culinary delights in the British Isles as a major preoccupation of the high-falutin section of the populace is added to by the following thought. If you knew of a good cheap place where they fed you well would you advertise it? Only if you were "public spirited". And if you were that kind of do-gooder you would undoubtedly end up as "a Burmese fish curry" (South Petherton), or as "chastely steamed broccoli" (Cheltenham), served on flagstones with cagefuls of stuffed birds about you. Serve you right.

The Good Food Guide 1981, *ed. C. Driver (first published 1951 and thereafter annually) Consumers' Association, Hodder and Stoughton*

ROBERT WATERHOUSE
Vanity Mirror

Professor Banham in *Los Angeles: the Architecture of the Four Ecologies* tells us that he learnt to drive a motor car to discover Los Angeles. It's like saying one learns to read to sample Shakespeare. The idea of the unsullied prof snapping off his bicycle clips and slipping on his sneakers to take the wheel of a powerglide creaming up Sunset Boulevard hardly fills one with confidence about the judgments which this middle-aged whizz-kid prophet has in store.

Of course, Reyner is not simply setting out to sing the praises of a then-unfashionable metropolis. He wants to do a demolition job on conventional planning wisdom stemming, as he puts it, from the Futurists and Le Corbusier to Jane Jacobs and Sibyl Moholy-Nagy: namely that cities thrive on density and diversity. Los Angeles, patently loose-limbed, far-stretched, without much of a recognisable centre, nonetheless "performs the function of a great city in terms of size, cosmopolitan style, creative energy, international influence, distinctive way of life and corporate personality".

So what? LA is a great city. Planes fly there from all over the world. People flock there. Like it or not, it's the centre of the most affluent state in the world's most powerful nation. Imagine California without LA . . . But creative energy, cosmopolitan style, international influence? Not really.

And what's all this about four ecologies (the very use of the word is subversive, since ecology in England at least tends to refer to benign practices vis-à-vis the world's natural resources)? Ah, yes. The ecology of "Surfurbia", the surfers' paradise cum dormitory township; the ecology of the foothills, into which LA has ploughed relentlessly and unimaginatively; the ecology of the Plains of Id, LA's central flatlands, or badlands;

and the ecology of Autopia. No, not death by asphyxiation, just car-madness.

Let the man himself take up the story. "The first time I saw it happen nothing registered on my conscious mind, because it all seemed so natural – as the car in front turned down the off-ramp of the San Diego freeway, the girl beside the driver pulled down the sun-visor and used the mirror on the back of it to tidy her hair. Only when I had seen a couple more incidents of the kind did I catch their import: that coming off the freeway is coming in from outdoors."

Indeed. That's what vanity mirrors are for, I would have thought, tidying hair. You can't see through your rear window with them.

The sad thing about Reyner's ecologies is that they prove so insubstantial, and they don't manage to include much architecture, the one place where the professor is on firm ground. That means he has to add another chapter, called an Ecology for Architecture, putting the few tangible achievements in the context of "a great dream, the dream of the urban homestead, the dream of a good life outside the squalors of the European type of city". LA, to Prof Banham, is excused its mile after boring mile because there are few urban poor and because there is "room to swing the proverbial cat".

Reyner ends with a list of the architectural and urban design achievements of this great city as if, pathetically, trying to justify his stance by the very standards of the conventional wisdom he despises. Pretty small the list is, too, for such a huge place. Rather than searching for highlights, should not Banham have celebrated the tawdry, repetitive quality of the LA townscape as the logical expression of modern man's spiritual bankruptcy?

Reyner Banham, Los Angeles: The Architecture of Four Ecologies *(first published 1971), Penguin, 1973*

HARRY WHEWELL
Thought, Word and Deed

Its very title bespeaks a naivety bordering on the ludicrous, and the same humourlessness is stamped on every page. So, more importantly, is a simplistic view of the world which is irrelevant when it is not downright wrong-headed and misleading.

Scouting for Boys, Baden-Powell's Bible for the Boy Scouts, was not published in Britain until 1932, but it was written in his head thirty years before then when he was on the other side of the world in South Africa during the Boer War. The idea for the movement came out of the siege of Mafeking. As its founder explains in his book: "Lord Edward Cecil, the chief staff officer, gathered together the boys of Mafeking and made them into a cadet corps. He put them in uniform and drilled them. And a jolly smart and useful lot they were."

If the thought ever occurred to Baden-Powell that such a cadet corps might need adapting in one or two particulars to meet the needs of boys living in British cities during the 1920s and 1930s he brushed it away.

And so there grew up tens of thousands of boys whose main influence outside the home was a movement which dressed its members in a uniform "very like the uniform worn by my men when I commanded the South African Constabulary", and gave them a manual which taught them how to stop runaway horses, how to light fires with wet matches, how to span ravines with rope bridges, and how to stalk an emu "with a boomerang in the hand and a spear between the toes".

Some would say that if this did them no great good it did them no great harm either. But can the same be said for the advice which *Scouting for Boys* offers on deeper matters? A chapter headed "Continence" has this to say: "Some boys, like those who start smoking, think it is a very fine and manly thing to tell or listen to dirty stories, but it only shows them to be little fools. Yet such talk or the reading of trashy books or looking at lewd pictures are very apt to lead a thoughtless boy into the temptation of masturbation. This tends to lower both health and spirits. But if you have any manliness in you you will throw off such temptation at once."

Then there are these pointers to assessing other people. "The way a man walks is often a good guide to his character – witness the fussy, swaggering little man paddling along with short steps, with much arm action; the nervous man's hurried, jerky stride; the slow slough of the loafer; the smooth, quick and silent step of the Scout, and so on." Finally, towards the end of the book, under the heading "Choose a Career", comes this gem which must have rung as hollowly in the 1930s as it does today. "An employer told me once that he never engaged a lad who had yellow fingertips (from smoking) or who carried his mouth open (boys who breathe through their mouth have a stupid look). Any man is sure of employment who has money in the bank, keeps away from drink, and is cheery."

It is highly probable that one or two copies of *Scouting for Boys* did go down with the Titanic. It might have been better if all of them had. In fact, the work, subtitled, "A Handbook for Instruction in Good Citizenship", went on through thirty-four editions. The last I can trace was a reprint in 1974, and it is from this that all my quotations have been taken.

Lord Robert Stephenson Smythe Baden-Powell, Scouting for Boys *(first published 1932), Scout Association, 1974*

CHARLES WOOD
The Unkindest Cut

Mabel Maple, attractive, late forties, swings her once lovely legs up on to the grotty sofa in a once luxurious suite at the Chateau Marmont, 8221 Sunset Boulevard, Hollywood, California, puts down her book, takes off her reading glasses and says to her husband the little known screenwriter Gordon Maple, fat, balding, grey, ill, harassed, legs twisted sugarstick under nasty paper laden modern table, earlier forties than his wife but getting minute by minute older, "Hey, stop typing or you'll make yourself ill again!" He doesn't. He is going into a glazed look. She shouts at him, "Hi Honey!" He says, "Electric typewriters are intelligent, warm, sexy and they hum soothingly, unlike wives."

"Stop typing and relax, think of something else."

"Such as?"

"Such as which book do you hate more than any other in the world?" Quick as a flash, Gordon answers, "*Vile Bodies.*" "Yes", says Mabel with great understanding, "I know you hate *Vile Bodies* at the moment but which book do you really hate more than any other?"

"Why? Has somebody sent me one?" Then cagily, Gordon asks again, "Why?"

"Because I want to know. There was somebody in the lift, tall, thin, pale, early thirties, worried, wearing jeans, talking about it."

"Who?"

"I don't know, but he was English."

"Christopher Hampton's here. Was it him? They're all here, that lot, Wilson Snoodle, that lot, the place is crawling with them, clattering with them, listen . . .!" They listen. Mabel Maple can't hear anything for the wail of the hookers on the Strip and the keening of the impotent police cars, "Hi Honey? Hi Honey? Leave the County or go to Jail! Whaa Whaaa, Whaaa, Whaaa,

Whop Whop Whop!" She says so. Gordon can hear a typewriter in action, no two, three, distinct working typewriters. She can't. "Anyway, just to get your mind off your film for a moment, in the lift they were talking about the book they hated most."

Gordon shouts, "*Vile Bodies, Vile Bodies, Vile Bodies* by Evelyn Waugh!" and chokes on his Perrier.

"You didn't say that when the nice producer gentleman asked you to adapt it for a major motion picture, you said you thought it was marvellous and very funny and *would* make a major motion picture, and then you said you would do it, and then you thought you ought to read it and borrowed it from Kate and actually did like it and cried triumphantly, 'This will make a major motion picture', and . . . there's a roll of kitchen paper on the gas stove, no there isn't, I'll get you some from the loo, don't use your bathing trunks . . . will it harm the typewriter? Shouldn't you switch off the electricity before you touch wet paper in an electric typewriter? I say, aren't they good? Did you not even get a tingle right up your arm? I say, half a bottle of Perrier in the works and still it works, hums, just like you." Tasting from the glass he has been using she exclaims, "This isn't Perrier! It's Californian plonk."

"It's some Perrier, mostly Perrier on top."

"Aaah, the light is blinking, does that mean you're telling a lie, because it's true?" "Which light?" "The light on the typewriter," says Mabel. "Oh, that, it's always done that, I find it comforting," says Gordon affectionately. "Are you sure it has? Are you sure there wasn't a tremble?" "You mean tremor, and no there wasn't one." "Are you sure?" "Yes, but it is odd that everywhere we go there are earthquake warnings, have you noticed that Mabel?"

"Gordon Maple, we are four floors up in the jerriest built building in the jerriest built city in America!"

"Yes, I'm sorry about that, but Bogart slept here you know, and Nicholas Ray worked in one of the bungalows, and if you lean out you can see where the Garden of Allah used to be, I mean faded glory, charm, curtains . . . There's a lady up there, on the balcony above your head without a stitch on!" "I knew you'd notice that," says Mabel. "I wasn't going to tell you until you'd finished typing, your work, but now you know." "She would have gone by then, Mabel." "That's quite possible, they do go in when the sun goes down." "Actually," Gordon admits, "I saw her yesterday, at least I didn't, Jerzy did, when he came to talk, apparently they're here for the Oscars. He walked in, you know what he's like, you were down at the pool, you know what he's like with his neat shoes and his blink, he looked up and said did I realise there was a lady without any clothes on against the sky, and I quick as a flash, Gordon, which I am, said that I knew and that she was here for the Oscars, that was shortly before we knew Reagan had got shot, but when we did, she went in and put some clothes on, the least she could do I suppose, anyway now she's back, apparently he's out of danger, so, off come the nicks again . . . pubic hair is very in, in LA."

"Not down at the pool it isn't, and don't think she didn't know that Jerzy was here, that he's a producer." "How would she know that?" "They do, they do . . ."

"Nobody ever takes their clothes off for writers," says Gordon sadly. "Have you noticed?"

"I do".

"You are obliged to, in order to get into bed with one . . . I mean other women, girls . . . but let it be known you are a producer and they're out of their boiler suits at once, aren't they?"

"Good lord!"

"Yes, I wondered when you'd notice him, he was there yesterday too, he's come for the Oscars, you can see why he's a star, can't you?"

"He won't get it."

"What?"

"Best actor." "Oh, I don't know, it all depends on the part you know, that's what's wrong with *Vile Bodies* as a major motion picture book, the parts aren't sympathetic enough for a present-day American audience, they like to root for someone, that's why it's a rotten book, nobody to root for. Take Adam for instance, Adam is wet. Now nobody is as wet as Adam, I mean slaving over his memoirs for a whole week in Paris and then having them burned by Customs and doing absolutely nothing about it, wet. And what kind of a background does he have? Is he a fully rounded character, you have to have them fully rounded, is he? I mean not in the book he isn't, is he? Well I've done my best to fully round him, given him 'street' credibility with a deprived childhood and a North Country accent, which incidentally has solved the problem of where to find a young actor who can actually talk like a gent these days now that they don't learn it in weekly rep any more; and, stroke of genius he has a limp which was caused by a plastic bullet, though they didn't have those then, shot at him by Winston Churchill when our Adam Activist-Symes was leading the South Wales miners, but will that be enough in the face of the overall Waugh wetness and lack of grasping the nettle of the times, and what is more will the youth of today identify with this chap who spends all his time going to parties and falling asleep and never being able to stand up for his rights, and always in debt and not saying a word in protest when the whole of his life in memoirs-oblique-literary-oblique-five hundred-pages-of-closely-written-typescript-terms goes up in flames at HM Customs, at the whim of a very low grade, you can tell by the way he talks, Customs Officer? Shocking grammar, I've looked up Customs Officers, done Waugh's research for him and they had to pass exams you know, Customs Officers, they wouldn't have said things like, 'Have you wore them?' to young ladies called Chastity, while going through her things, no, 'Have you worn them?', would have been the line, and what about the sex? I don't find the sex true to life, I really don't, and there is nothing to laugh about in young girls called Chastity being sent to South America to pleasure old men, Jody Foster type, though we won't be able to get her, she's too big now, mind you so is chastity now, very big and getting bigger so I'm told, there's a promiscuity backlash on the campus I'm told, saw it on the television this morning very early, mind you I do distinctly remember, very late last night, you had gone to bed but I stayed up to watch the hookers down on the Strip and Peter O'Toole talking about *Masada*, and of course went straight to sleep but woke up and I distinctly heard a very learned Doctor of something talking about masturbating with a notched cucumber, and do you know, I accepted it? Adjusted my clothes and nodding sympathetically staggered off to bed where I found you and told you what I had just heard and you said, 'Breakfast television, it will never work,' and went off to sleep again. Then there's his attitude to race, a Jesuit called Rothschild, very naughty and totally untrue, there would never have been one, never, and just you try and get away with that in America, and what am I going to do about 'nigger'? It is said, yes it is said, we are thinking of changing it to 'Indian' in the best Agatha Christie tradition. All these things can be licked of course and I'm doing my best, but the main stumbling block remains Adam and his wetness and lack of balls, we'll never be able to cast it unless John Hurt gets Best Actor and he's too old, we all went to look at him in that restaurant yesterday and decided, he sends his love to you."

"But he doesn't know me," says Mabel.

"I know, he doesn't know me either," says Gordon, adding, "but they're here for the Oscars, you know how it is."

A knock on the door. Mabel goes, comes back with a sheet of paper in her hand. There is a smiling Mexican at the door, fifties, full head of hair, lean, tough, handsome, sloppy jeans, tartan shirt, hand flickering in and out like a reptile's tongue.

"He's found it."

"What?" "The page of script which blew out of the window the other day, you had them beating the undergrowth for it, he found it up a palm tree, will five dollars be enough?" "Oh yes."

Gordon looks at the sheet of paper, winces, looks more intently, says, "I didn't write this!"

"Yes, you did, it's Adam and Nina, look," says Mabel pointing out the characters. "Yes, I know, but this is straight from the book, line for line," says Gordon.

"It's very funny," laughs Mabel, reading from the

sheet of paper. "I'm sure it is, I'm sure it is, straight from the book, word for word," shouts Gordon. "I didn't write that."

"Oh."

"Quite, there's somebody else writing that, in this very hotel, somebody else, of course it's funny, it's a very funny book . . . the bastards, they've hired two of us!"

"Never mind, darling, perhaps they'll choose your version, you have put a lot of yourself into it," says Mabel consolingly.

"And what's more, they've put him in a penthouse, haven't they, up there, perhaps it's him, up there with his naked lady, I mean found in a palm tree, I'm not high enough up for that . . . yes, that's him . . . writing my book . . . he must have a word processor, and that's his secretary . . .!"

"No, darling, I can see from here, that is not the attitude of a writer," says Mabel sadly. "Perhaps you wrote it in your sleep?"

Charles Wood created the characters Gordon and Mabel Maple for the television series *Don't Forget to Write*

Evelyn Waugh, Vile Bodies *(first published 1930), Penguin, 1970*

IAN WOOLDRIDGE
Slant-Eyed Oriental

When Mister Redhead rote askin would you like to ern a few quid sayin wot is the rottenest book you have ever read I was somewhat flattered becoz most interlectuals reckon that us sportswriters is too busy falling over in bars to have ever herd of Albert Hemingway and that.

Anyway first of all I was going to give the red card to *Silas Marner* which is all about some miserabul skinflint pedofile-suspect but that was mainly becoz I had to lern it by heart in the days when O-levels was called Skool Cert and English teachers wot hadn't been called up for the war was so upset at not bein killed that they swore blind to give grubby irchins like me a lifelong hatred of books.

Then, on sekond thoughts, I thought about awardin the black spot to *Olympic Greats* mostly becoz the New Zealand bloke wot rote it seemed to have done wot is known in Fleet Street as a "cuttings job".

A "cuttings job" means that you sit in a warm office with a bloody great pile of newspaper cuttings and al! you do is re-rite facts gathered by sportsriters like me wot spend their miserabul lives hanging around dressing rooms and Novosibirsk airport and gettin arrested in Zaire and Buenos Aires at a cost of millions of quids to our newspapers only to find later that this bloke who never moves off his ass in London nicks all yore inform-ashun and presents it in hard covers under his own name as though he actually knew the people wot you was riting about.

Nasty bisness, really, but I suddenly realised that this New Zealand bloke mite be bigger than me and thus gave it the elbow.

So we defnitly come to the daftest book ever ritten which is called *The Sixth Congress of the Workers' Party of Korea on the Work of the Central Committee* by a slant-eyed nutter called Kim Il Sung, which may sound like the name of the second favourite at Hong Kong races but is acktualy the boss-man of North Korea and therefor the world's longest-raining diktater.

Listen to this:

> To provide complete independence to the working masses it is necessary to clear away the remnants of the old society from all spheres of social life including politics, the economy, ideology and culture and emancipate the working people from all kinds of domination, subordination and social inequality.

So it raves on, beautifully bound in red rexine with gold in-laid lettring, for 119 pages saying the same fing over and over again.

Well, wot a larf, honerstly, becoz if you've ever been to Pyongyang, which you haven't, you'd know that it makes Moscow feel like New Orleens. The poor bastards wot are born there have got to stay there wearin illuminated badges of Kim Il Sung's face on identikal suits and hopin that if they work like niggers and keep their noses cleen for thirty years they mite get a permit wot allows them to borrow a state-owned bike to get to work in the paddy fields on.

The only reeson I know this is that I went to North Korea once to rite about a table tenis match. Normally they shoot all visitors and pertikularly jernalists on site but they rekoned it was okay to let a few sportsriters in bekoz they're mostly too stupid or drunk to distingwish ideolojical brainwashing from a topspun forehand smash.

Anyway ever since I went there they have been sending me these books by Kim Il Sung. I shall now rite back and tell them that I have nomernated *The Sixth Congress of the Workers' Party of Korea on the Work of the Central Committee* for Mr Redhead of *Today* fame's speshal litry award and I expect they will be very pleased.

PS. Is that enuff? PPS. I hesirtate about riting any more about Korea in case that New Zealand bloke nicks it for a 600-page exklusive book about Korean culture and that. Yours in sport.

George Eliot, Silas Marner *(first published 1861), OUP, 1979*
Kim Il Sung, The Sixth Congress of the Workers' Party of
Korea on the Work of the Central Committee
(first published 1975)

ONE MAN'S MEAT ...

The ten most uncherished books of all

We asked our contributors – and the readers of a Sunday newspaper – to send us lists of their ten least-liked books of all time. The answers contained some surprises. Richardson, Scott, Melville and Hermann Broch (all of whom rank high on the editors' own hit list) managed only one vote each. Proust, Tolstoy and Dostoievsky (often savaged in conversation) escaped unscathed. The Old Testament roused only one man's wrath, and even he quite liked the Psalms.

One contributor hurled malice in handfuls. "I'd nominate any hand-tinted diary done in 1903 and expensively published now." "I'd pulp all books with titles like *Uruguayan Poetry Today*." "Who needs to know about *The Making of the President* — any president?" "Let's burn all books of lists, starting with this one." Another contributor asked "As a special favour could the above books be disposed of with a bonfire of all extant scores and records of Stravinsky, ignited by Blake's pictures?" Steady, now ...

Anyone browsing in the library of the Towering Inferno will find it amply stocked with Complete Works: Kingsley Amis, Pam Ayres, Byron, Camus, Compton-Burnett, Conan Doyle, Margaret Drabble, George Eliot, Faulkner, Marilyn French, Paul Gallico, Sagan and Sartre. The children's shelves groan with *Little Women*, *Uncle Tom's Cabin*, the *Noddy* books, *Lamb's Tales from Shakespeare* and *Eric (or Little by Little)*. A whole non-fiction wing houses everything from the *Bhagavad Gita*, Casanova's *Memoirs* and Plutarch's *Lives* to Samuel Smiles' *Self-help*, Masters and Johnson's *Human Sexual Inadequacy* and (no connection) Gay Talese's *Thy Neighbour's Wife*. Edmund Wilson (*The Twenties*), Colin Wilson (*The Outsider*) and Harold Wilson (*The Diaries*) lie side by side, gazing across the shelves at Gurdjieff and Hitler, Keynes and Kissinger, Arthur Schlesinger and Ezra Pound.

In the fiction bay, some of the choices may raise eyebrows. What irrepressible bile, for example, makes men turn on Doctorow's *Ragtime*, Irving's *Garp*, or the novels of Heller, Hemingway and Hesse? Are Meredith's *The Amazing Marriage*, Manning's *Her Privates We* and Pater's *Marius the Epicurean* really as bad as people say? Grass, Mann, Pasternak, Solzhenitsyn, Updike – the list contains most novelists of stature read today. Should fiction-writers *not* in the Loathly Library not bite their lips?

The ten most favoured candidates for oblivion, each with several sponsors, were these. (We give them in alphabetical order, but an outspoken novelist, a writer of fantasy and a politician tied for first place.)

Ten books for the bottom line:

William Faulkner, Requiem for a Nun *(first published 1953),* Penguin, *1970*

Gustave Flaubert, Salammbô *(first published 1862), Penguin,* 1977

John Fowles, The Magus *(first published 1966), Panther,* 1978

The Good Food Guide *(first published 1951 and thereafter annually) Consumers' Association, Hodder and Stoughton,* 1981, ed. C. Driver

Adolf Hitler, Mein Kampf *(first published 1925-6), Hutchinson,* 1972

James Joyce, Finnegans Wake *(first published 1939), Faber,* 1975

D. H. Lawrence, Women in Love *(first published 1921),* Penguin, *1969*

The New English Bible *(first published 1961), CUP, 1970*

J. R. R. Tolkien, The Lord of the Rings *(first published 1954-5), Allen and Unwin, 1979*

Harold Wilson, The Governance of Britain *(first published 1976), Sphere, 1977*

BIOGRAPHICAL DETAIL

JEFFREY ARCHER was Conservative MP for Louth, 1969–74. His books include *Not a Penny More, Not a Penny Less; Shall We Tell the President* and *Kane and Abel*.

BERYL BAINBRIDGE is a novelist and playwright. Her books include *Harriet Said . . .; The Bottle Factory Outing; Injury Time* and *Young Adolf*.

PATRICIA BEER is a poet and critic. Her *Selected Poems* were published in 1979.

DIANA BISHOP is an actress and poet. Her most recent book is a translation of the French poet Jean Tardieu.

BASIL BOOTHROYD, over forty years a *Punch* contributor, has published sixteen books of humour and an official life of Prince Philip.

CAROLINE CONRAN is *The Sunday Times* cookery correspondent. Her recent books include *The Cook Book* with Terence Conran, the English edition of the Troisgros Brothers' *Nouvelle Cuisine* and *British Cooking*.

ALAN COREN is the editor of *Punch*. His books include *The Sanity Inspector; The Bulletins of Idi Amin; Golfing for Cats* and his latest, *Tissues for Men*.

RUSSELL DAVIES is the TV critic of *The Sunday Times* and illustrator of *The Improved Version of Peregrine Prykke's Pilgrimage Through the Literary World*.

FRANK DELANEY is the presenter of *Bookshelf* on BBC Radio 4. His most recent book is *James Joyce's Odyssey: A Guide to the Dublin of Ulysses*.

JANICE ELLIOTT is an author and journalist. Her novels include *The Honey Tree; Summer People* and *Secret Places*.

MICHAEL GREEN is a journalist and author, writer of the "Coarse" series: *Coarse Rugby; Coarse Acting; Coarse Moving* and *Coarse Sex,* among others.

ALEX HAMILTON writes on literary matters for *The Guardian.* His own books include *As If She Were Mine; Wild Track; Town Parole* and *Beam of Malice.*

TIM HEALD is a journalist, a novelist (the "Simon Bognor" crime series) and a biographer; among his most recent books is *HRH: The Man who will be King.*

ROBERT HELLER is a journalist, broadcaster and author. His books include *The Naked Manager* and, more recently, *The Naked Investor; The Once and Future Manager; The Business of Winning* and *Food for Work.*

BEVIS HILLIER, formerly editor of *The Connoisseur* and author of many books, including *Art Deco; Pottery and Porcelain 1700-1914* and *Austerity Binge,* is currently writing the authorised life of Sir John Betjeman.

MICHAEL HOLROYD is an author and biographer. His books include biographies of Lytton Strachey and Augustus John, and a symposium, *The Genius of Shaw.*

ROLAND HUNTFORD was formerly the Scandinavian correspondent of *The Observer.* His books include *Sea of Darkness; Scott and Amundsen* and *The New Totalitarians.*

BRIAN INGLIS was editor of *The Spectator,* 1959-62, and presenter of the television series *All Our Yesterdays.* His books include *A History of Medicine; Natural and Supernatural* and *The Diseases of Civilisation.*

DAVID IRVING is a historian. His books include *The Rise and Fall of the Luftwaffe; Rommel; Hitler's War* and *Uprising!*

D. A. N. JONES is assistant editor of *The Listener.* His books include the novels *Parade in Paris* and *Never Had it so Good.*

H. R. F. KEATING is the crime reviewer for *The Times* and the author of many novels including *The Murder of the Maharajah; A Long Walk to Wimbledon* and the "Inspector Ghote" series.

MILES KINGTON is a journalist, humorous writer and musician (one quarter of Instant Sunshine). His latest book is *Let's Parler Franglais*.

PAUL LEVY writes for *The Observer*. His books include *Moore* and, with Michael Holroyd, *The Shorter Strachey*.

GEORGE MACBETH is a poet and editor (notably of *Poetry Now*, 1965-76). His books include *A Doomsday Book; A Poet's Year* and *Poems of Love and Death*.

FAY MASCHLER writes the restaurant column on the *New Standard*. She has written many books including *Cooking is a Game You Can Eat*.

SHERIDAN MORLEY is drama critic and arts editor of *Punch* and London theatre critic for the *International Herald Tribune*; he also writes regularly for *The Times* and is a frequent broadcaster. His biographies include *Oscar Wilde, Noel Coward, Gertrude Lawrence* and *Gladys Cooper*.

CHARLES OSBORNE is Literature Director of the Arts Council of Great Britain, and the author of several books on literary and musical subjects, the most recent of which is *W. H. Auden: The Life of a Poet*.

JOHN OSBORNE is a playwright. His works include *Look Back In Anger; The Entertainer; Inadmissible Evidence* and *Luther*.

STEVE RACE is a musician and broadcaster, question-master of the television and radio programme *My Music*. His book, *Dear Music Lover*, was recently published.

FREDERIC RAPHAEL is a novelist and screenwriter. His novels include *Lindmann; April, June and November* and *California Time*. He wrote the screenplays for *Two For The Road, The Glittering Prizes* and *Richard's Things*. He writes regularly for *The Sunday Times*.

STANLEY REYNOLDS is the literary editor of *Punch*. He has written the novels *Better Dead Than Red* and *Thirty is a Dangerous Age Cynthia* and the musicals *Androcles and the Lion* and *Desolation Angel*.

HILARY RUBINSTEIN is a literary agent, broadcaster and writer, editor of *The Good Hotel Guide* and author of *The Complete Insomniac.*

MICHAEL SCHMIDT is a publisher, writer and broadcaster. His books include *A Change of Affairs* (poems), *The Colonist* (novel) and *50 Poets from Gower to Hopkins.*

AUDREY SLAUGHTER is a journalist who worked on *The Sunday Times* from 1979-81 and is now an associate editor on the *Sunday Express Magazine.*

ANNE SMITH is the founder and editor of *The Literary Review.* Her most recent book is the novel *The Magic Glass.*

ANTHONY SMITH is an author and broadcaster, and creator of *A Sideways Look* on BBC Radio 4. His books include *Blind White Fish in Persia; Throw Out Two Hands* and *The Body.*

GODFREY SMITH writes for *The Sunday Times.* His books include *Caviare* and *Best of Nathaniel Gubbins* (ed.).

JOHN TIMPSON is a journalist and broadcaster, a presenter of the *Today* programme on BBC Radio 4.

PETER TINNISWOOD is a novelist and playwright. His books include *A Touch of Daniel; I Didn't Know You Cared* and *Shemerelda.* He is the author of the plays, *Wilfred; The Day War Broke Out* and *You Should See Us Now,*

POLLY TOYNBEE is a columnist on *The Guardian.* Her documentary books include *A Working Life* and *Hospital.*

JOHN VAIZEY is a writer, an economist and a member of the House of Lords. Among his most recent publications is *Capitalism and Socialism* and *The Squandered Peace* is soon to be published.

ROBERT WATERHOUSE, a freelance journalist, is the founder and editor of *The Withington Reporter.*

HARRY WHEWELL is Northern editor of *The Guardian.*

CHARLES WOOD is a screenwriter — *The Knack; Help! The*

Long Day's Dying; How I Won The War; The Charge of the Light Brigade and *Cuba.*

IAN WOOLDRIDGE writes on sport for *The Daily Mail.*

INDEX OF AUTHORS AND TITLES

Chief entries are shown in **bold type**

Across the River and Into the Trees, 82, 83
Afternoon at the Seaside, 17
Akhnaton, 17
Alice's Adventures in Wonderland, 74, 75
Amazing Marriage, The, 123
Amis Kingsley, **122**
Amis, Martin, 57
Atkins, Robert C., 9, 10
Ayres, Pam, 122

Baden-Powell, Robert, 112, 113
Balzac, Honoré de, 36, 37
Banham, Reyner, 110, 111
Bennett, Arnold, 79
Bhagavad Gita, 58, 122
Bible, The, 74, 75, 84
Big Six, The, 42
Boccaccio, Giovanni, 27
Book of Leviticus, The, 84, 85
Book of Martyrs (Foxe's), 91, 93
Borradaile, Eastham, Potts and Saunders, 95
Broch, Hermann, 122
Brophy, B., Levey, M. and Osborne, C., 68
Byron, George, 122

Cage and Aviary Birds, 102, 103
Camus, Albert, 122
Captain Horation Ramage, 30
Carroll, Lewis, 74, 75
Cartland, Barbara, 91, 92, 93
Casanova, Giovanni Giacomo, 122
Christie, Agatha, 15, 16, 17
Cleland, John, 27
Comédie Humaine, La, 36, 37
Complete Scarsdale Medical Diet, 32, 33
Compton-Burnett, Ivy, 122
Conan Doyle, Arthur, 122

Concise Oxford Dictionary, The, 9, 10
Conran, Shirley, 106
Coot Club, 41, 42
Country Diary of an Edwardian Lady, 9, 10
Couples, 27

Dance to the Music of Time, A, 7
Decline and Fall of the Roman Empire, The, 19
Diaries (Harold Wilson's), 122
Diary of a Nobody, The, 38, 40
Dickens, Charles, 37, 38, 40
Didion, Joan, 20, 21
Dr Atkins' Diet Revolution, 9, 10
Doctorow, Ed, 123
Dostoievsky, Fyodor, 122
Drabble, Margaret, 122
Driver, Christopher, 109, 123

Eliot, George, 121, 122
Encyclopaedia Britannica, 60
Eric (or Little by Little), 122

Farewell to Arms, A, 61, 62, 63, 82, 83
Farrell, J. T., 93
Faulkner, William, 122, 123
Fear of Flying, 27
Female Eunuch, The, 20, 21
Fest, Joachim, 47, 48
Fiesta, 61, 63, 82, 83
Fifty Works of English Literature We Could Do Without, 68
Finnegans Wake, 25, 41, 123
Flaubert, Gustave, 123
For Whom the Bell Tolls, 82, 83
Fowles, John, 123
Foxe, Dean, 91, 93
Fraser, Antonia, 53, 55, 56
Frazer, James, 45, 46
French, Marilyn, 122
Freud, Sigmund, 11, 12, 43, 44

Gallico, Paul, 122
Garp, 123
Gibbon, Edward, 19
Gide, André, 86, 87
Girl Guide Handbook, The, 104

Godfather, The, 36, 37
Golden Bough, The, 45, 46
Good Food Guide, The, 107, 109, 123
Governance of Britain, The, 123
Grahame, Kenneth, 75
Grass, Günther, 123
Greer, Germaine, 20, 21
Grossmith George and Weedon, 38, 39, 40
Guinness Book of Records, The, 66, 67
Gurdjieff, Georg Ivanovich, 59, 123

Hall, Radclyffe, 27
Harris, Frank, 27
Hell-cat and the King, The, 91, 92, 93
Heller, Joseph, 123
Hemingway, Ernest, 61, 62, 63, 83, 123
Henry Root Letters, The, 9, 10
Her Privates We, 123
Hesse, Hermann, 123
Higher School Inorganic Chemistry, 95
Hitler, 47, 48
Hitler, Adolf, 95, 123
Holden, Edith, 10
Holmyard, Q.E.D., 95
House at Pooh Corner, The, 74, 75
Human Sexual Inadequacy, 122

I Ching, 20
Immoraliste, L', 86, 87
In Sickness and in Health, 10
In the Mink, 88, 89, 90
Intermediate Physics, 95
Interpretation of Dreams, The, 11, 12
Invertebrata, The, 95
Irving, John, 123

James Bond's Moonraker, 59
Jong, Erica, 8, 27
Joyce, James, 25, 123

Kafka, Franz, 86
Keating, H. R. F., 52
Keynes, John Maynard, 123
Kim Il Sung, 120, 121
King Arthur and the Knights of the Round Table, 53, 56
Kissinger, Henry, 123

Lady Chatterley's Lover, 26, 27, 92
Lamb's Tales from Shakespeare, 122
Lang, Andrew, 45, 46
Lawrence, D. H., 26, 27, 91, 93, 123
Lawrence, T. E., 18, 19
Laws, The, 77, 78
Leavis, F. R., 13, 14
Levey, Michael, 68
Lion and the Unicorn, The, 49, 50
Little Women, 122
Lives (Plutarch's), 122
Lolita, 7
London Telephone Directory, The, 60
Lord of the Rings, The, 7, 123
Los Angeles: the Architecture of the Four Ecologies, 110, 111

McWhirter, N. D., 67
Magic and Religion, 45, 46
Magus, The, 123
Mailer, Norman, 27, 62
Making of the President, The, 122
Mann, Thomas, 86, 123
Manning, Frederic, 123
Marius the Epicurean, 123
Martin, Richard Mark, 102, 103
Masters, W. H. and Johnson, V.E., 122
Mein Kampf, 94, 95, 123
Melvilie, Herman, 122
Memoirs (Casanova's), 122
Meredith, George, 123
Middlemarch, 59
Miller, Henry, 11, 12, 27, 62, 83
Millett, Kate, 62, 63
Milne, A. A., 75
Missee Lee, 42
Mousetrap, The, 17
Murder is Announced, A, 17
Murder on the Nile, 17
Murray, Margaret, 46

Nabokov, Vladimir, 7, 70, 71, 72, 73
Ned Kelly, 68, 69
New Bearings in English Poetry, 13, 14
New English Bible, The, 23, 123

Nicolson, Nigel, 98
Noddy (etc), 122

O'Brien, Edna, 27
"O'Forester, Dudley", 30
Old Man and the Sea, The, 61, 63
Old Testament, The, 122
Olympic Greats, 120
Orwell, George, 49, 50
Osborne, Charles, 68, 69
Outsider, The, 122
Owen, David, 9, 10
Oxford English Dictionary, The, 9, 10, 59

Pale Fire, 70, 71, 73
Pasternak, Boris, 123
Pater, Walter, 123
Perfect Murder, The, 52
Peter Duck, 42
Pickwick Papers, The, 40
Picts and the Martyrs, The, 42
Pigeon Post, 41, 42
Plato, 76, 77, 78
Plexus, 11, 12
Plutarch, 122
Pocket Oxford Dictionary, 9
Portrait of a Marriage, 98
Pound, Ezra, 123
Powell, Anthony, 7
Pritikin, Nathan, 64, 65
Pritikin Program for Diet and Exercise, The, 64, 65
Proust, Marcel, 122
Puzo, Mario, 36, 37

Ragtime, 123
Ransome, Arthur, 41, 42
Republic, The, 76, 77, 78
Requiem for a Nun, 123
Richardson, Samuel, 122
Robbins, Harold, 27
Roget, Peter Mark, 99, 101

Sackville-West, Vita, 97, 98
Sagan, Françoise, 122
Salammbô, 123

Sartre, Jean-Paul, 122
Sayers, Dorothy L., 7
Schlesinger, Arthur, 123
Scott, Walter, 122
Scott-James, Anne, 88, 90
Scouting for Boys, 112, 113
Secret Water, 42
Self-Help, 122
Seven Pillars of Wisdom, The, 18, 19
Sexual Politics, 62, 63
Silas Marner, 120, 121
Sixth Congress of the Workers' Party of Korea, The,
  120, 121
Smiles, Samuel, 122
Smith, C. J., 95
Smith, Delia, 9, 10
Solzhenitsyn, Alexander, 123
Spider's Web, 17
Studs Lonigan, 91, 93
Sun Also Rises, The, 82, 83
Superwoman, 106
Swallowdale, 42
Swallows and Amazons, 41, 42

Talese, Gay, 122
Tarnower, Herman, 32, 33
Ten Little Niggers/Negroes/Indians, 17
Thesaurus of English Words and Phrases, 99, 100, 101
Thomas, Dylan, 73
Thy Neighbour's Wife, 122
To Have and Have Not, 62, 63
Tolkien, J.R.R., 7, 123
Tolstoy, Leo, 10, 19, 122
Totem and Taboo, 43, 44
Towards Zero, 17
Trespasser, The, 91, 92, 93
Twenties, The, 122

Uncle Tom's Cabin, 94, 122
Unexpected Guest, The, 17
Unified Health Service, A, 10
Updike, John, 27, 123
Uruguayan Poetry Today, 122

Vile Bodies, 114, 115, 116, 119

War and Peace, 9, 10, 18, 19
Waugh, Evelyn, 115, 119
Waves, The, 29
We Didn't Mean to Go to Sea, 42
White Album, The, 20, 21
Who's Who, 34, 35
Who's Who in Baton-Twirling, 60
Wilson, Colin, 122
Wilson, Edmund, 7, 122
Wilson, Harold, 122, 123
Wind in the Willows, The, 74, 75
Winter Holiday, 42
Witch-cult in Western Europe, The, 46
Witness for the Prosecution, 17
Women in Love, 123
Woolf, Virginia, 28, 57

Zola, Émile, 36

We are actively considering a sequel to the Anti-Book-list, trawling similar (or even murkier) depths. We should be very pleased to have your reactions, anti-reviews, or a straightforward list of the books you would parcel up and drop in the sea. Please use this page to send a list – or if you prefer not to tear it out, simply write to the editors at the address below.

Ten Least-liked Books

1. ....
2. ....
3. ....
4. ....
5. ....
6. ....
7. ....
8. ....
9. ....
10. ....

Name:

Address:

Brian Redhead and Kenneth McLeish, The Anti-Book-list, Hodder and Stoughton Ltd, 47 Bedford Square, London WC1B 3DP.